The R

A LITTLE BOOK OF POLITICAL STUPIDITY

This book is dedicated with love to my parents
Lyn and Viv and to my brother Matthew.

The Ruling Asses

A LITTLE BOOK OF POLITICAL STUPIDITY

Stephen Robins

With a Foreword by
Peter Hennessy

PRION

First published 2001 by
Prion Books
an imprint of the
Carlton Publishing Group
20 Mortimer Street
London W1T 3JW

This paperback, revised edition published 2005

10 9 8 7 6 5 4 3 2 1

ISBN 1-85375-572-9

A catalogue record of this book can be obtained from
the British Library

Printed in Great Britain by
Mackays

CONTENTS

Foreword

A

B

C

D

Debate – Decision-Making – Defeat
Defence Policy – Democracy – Disability
Disarmament – Discrimination – Discussion
Diversity – Doctors – Drugs

E

Economic Policy – Economy – Education
Elections – Electricity – Employment Relations
Enthusiasm – Environmental Issues – Equality
Ethics – Europe – Excuses – Expectations
Experiments

F

Facts – Family – Famine – Farming – Field Sports
Fishing – Food – Foreign Policy – Free Speech
Freedom – Future

G

Gas – Gender – Geography – Germany
Government – Grammar – Gratitude
Great Britain – Gun Control

H

Hawaii – Health – History – Holland – Holocaust
Homosexuality – Hooliganism – Hope – Housing
Human Beings – Human Life – Human Nature
Humility – Hungary

P

Pagers – Paranoia – Parenthood – Parliament
Party Conferences – Patience – Past – Peerages
Pensioners – Perseverance – Personal Experience
Personality – Poland – Police – Politicians
Politics – Poverty – Power – Praise – Predictions
Preparation – Presidency – Principles – Priorities
Prisons – Privatisation – Problems – Procreation
Progress – Promises – Protest – Proverbs
Public Opinion – Publicity

R

Racism – Rape – Reality – Rebellion – Recession
Religion – Respect – Reports – Resignation
Responsibility – Rights – Riots – Rivalry
Royalty – Rumours – Russia

S

Sackings – Scotland – Secrecy – Self-Belief – Sex
Shock – Silence – Sleaze – Sleep – Social Policy
Social Security – Society – Space Exploration
Spin – Sport – Statesmen – Statistics – Success
Succession – Suggestions – Support – Surprise

T

Tactics – Taxation – Technology – Terrorism
Texas – Threats – Trade – Tradition – Transport
Trust – Truth

U
Unemployment – Universities – Unity

V
Vice Presidency – Violence – Votes
Voting Systems

W
Wales – Warfare – Warnings – Weapons
Welfare State – Wisdom – Wives – Women
Work – World

Y
Youth

FOREWORD

For many years I have believed that the Speaker of the House of Commons should give each new Member of Parliament a copy of George Orwell's fabled 1946 essay *Politics and the English Language* which railed against the poverty of political discourse and warned its readers that not only does it 'become ugly and inaccurate because our thoughts are foolish but the slovenliness of our language makes it easier for us to have foolish thoughts.' I think now that Stephen Robins' collection should join Orwell in the welcoming pack of every M.P. For politicians flourish – and as on these pages – fall by their wordpower or lack of it. Labour Party leader, Hugh Gaitskell, used to talk about 'the subtle terrorism of words'.

Perhaps the greatest linguistic danger of the twenty and twenty-first centuries is hyper-market political language – over-familiar, thought-free cliché inflamed by exaggeration and driven by bogus passion. The tragedy is that when politicians try to break out of the standard, jaded constraints of routine political exchange, they fall into Stephen Robins' clutches!

He will not be short of material for future editions.

Peter Hennessy
Attlee Professor of Contemporary British History,
Queen Mary,
University of London

Mr Speaker, I withdraw my statement that half the Cabinet are asses. Half the Cabinet are not asses.

Benjamin Disraeli, Prime Minister

ABORIGINES

Do you still throw spears at each other?

Prince Philip to an Aboriginal tribesman

ABORTION

Abortion is advocated only by persons who have themselves been born.

President Ronald Reagan

Well, I – we have said, and the platform refers to this – that we will support a human life amendment. We do not say which human life amendment. There are a number of them. Most Americans understand the complexities of the issue of abortion. It is a very complex issue.

Vice President Dan Quayle

My pro-life position is I believe there's life. It's not necessarily based in religion. I think there's a life there, therefore the notion of life, liberty and pursuit of happiness.

President George W. Bush

ACHIEVEMENTS

We are not without accomplishment. We have managed to distribute poverty equally.

Nguyen Co Thach, Vietnamese
Foreign Minister

We shall reach greater and greater platitudes of achievement.

Mayor Richard J. Daley of Chicago

I think there were some differences, there's no question, and will still be. We're talking about a major, major situation here that requires constant work. But it was well worth it and there's much more to it than just this – I mean just these sixteen accomplishments or whatever. I mean, we've got a major rapport, relationship of economics, major in the security, and all of that, we should not lose sight of.

President George Bush, Sr.

It is indeed fitting that we gather here today to pay tribute to Abraham Lincoln, who was born in a log cabin that he built with his own hands.

President Ronald Reagan

ACTIVISTS

You can sum up what CND means in two
words – 'trust the Kremlin'.

Winston Churchill MP

If it takes a bloodbath, let's get it over with.
No more appeasement.

**President Ronald Reagan, on student-led
demonstrations against the Vietnam War**

ADOLESCENCE

It was just inebriating what Midland was all
about then.

**President George W. Bush, on growing up in
Midland, Texas**

ADVICE

Michael Heseltine should come out of the
woodwork, stop waving his plastic chickens
about, run up the flag-pole and see who
salutes.

**Sir John Banham, Director General of the
Confederation of British Industry**

The NUPE candidate should put her voice where her mouth is.

**Derek Hatton, Deputy Leader of
Liverpool City Council**

Judge a man not by his clothes, but by his wife's clothes.

Lord Dewar

AFFIRMATIVE ACTION

If affirmative action means what I just described, what I'm for, then I'm for it.

President George W. Bush

AFRICA

We spent a lot of time talking about Africa, as we should. Africa is a nation that suffers from incredible disease.

President George W. Bush

Bongo Bongo land.

Alan Clark MP, on Africa

AGE

I'm now in my 70th decade ...

Theresa Gorman

AGREEMENT

I am not quite certain what my right honourable friend said, but we hold precisely the same view.

Margaret Thatcher, Prime Minister

All the Cabinet Ministers sat around the table with their heads nodding like cuckoo clocks.

Enoch Powell MP

Our Cabinet is always unanimous – except when we disagree.

William Vander Zalm, Premier of British Columbia, Canada

Those who say that I am not in agreement
with the policy are, rightly or wrongly, quite
wrong.

William Whitelaw MP

I don't know what he means, but I disagree
with him.

President George Bush, Sr.

We were unanimous – in fact, everybody was
unanimous.

Eric Heffer MP

AIDS

The problem with AIDS is – you got it, you
die. So why are we spending money on the
issue?

**Lieutenant Governor Dennis Rehberg of
Montana**

We're concerned about AIDS inside our
White House – make no mistake about it.

President George W. Bush

Good Christian people will not catch AIDS.

Edwina Currie MP

There's a whole range of things we're doing with condoms.

Norman Fowler MP, commenting on AIDS prevention

AIR TRAVEL

I'm glad to be back on the terra cotta.

John Prescott MP, speaking to reporters as he stepped off a plane

Air travel efficiency would improve if more travellers started going to less popular places.

Vice President Dan Quayle

You have only to fly over it or go in a helicopter ...

Nicholas Ridley MP

To go round the world in a week, which I did the other day, is very exhausting.

Lord Glenarthur

ALTERNATIVES

Interviewer: In view of the various anomalies, are you examining alternatives?

William Whitelaw MP: We are examining alternative anomalies.

AMBITIONS

I want to wrong that right.

John Prescott MP

We must restore to Chicago all the good things it never had.

Mayor Richard J. Daley of Chicago

My goal is to renew American civilisation and redirect the fate of the human race.

Newt Gingrich, Speaker of the House of Representatives

Why has Jesus Christ so far not succeeded in inducing the world to follow his teachings? It is because he taught the ideal without devising any practical means of attaining it.

That is why I am proposing a practical scheme to carry out his aims.

President Woodrow Wilson

I have no ambition to govern men. It is a painful and thankless office.

President Thomas Jefferson

The thought of being President frightens me and I do not think I want the job.

Ronald Reagan, in 1973

I have an enormous personal ambition. I want to shift the entire planet. And I'm doing it. I am now a famous person. I represent real power.

Newt Gingrich, Speaker of the House of Representatives

I don't want to be leader of the party. I'm happy to be in the top dozen.

Margaret Thatcher MP, in 1974

I mean, like, hasn't everybody thought about becoming President for years?

George Bush, Sr., campaigning for the presidency

AMERICA

America is the only nation in history which miraculously has gone directly from barbarism to degeneration without the usual interval of civilisation.

Georges Clemenceau, French Politician

ANIMALS

I know the human being and fish can coexist peacefully.

President George W. Bush

I think I have a right to resent, to object to libellous statements about my dog.

President Franklin Roosevelt

Nobody's told me the difference between a red squirrel, a black one or a brown one. Do we have to save every subspecies?

Manuel Lujan, George Bush's Interior Secretary, on the Endangered Species Act

How on earth do the birds know it is a sanctuary?

Sir Keith Joseph MP, whilst visiting a bird sanctuary

No – I might catch some ghastly disease.

Prince Philip, upon being asked if he would like to stroke a koala bear

The left don't have a monopoly on ecology. We at the National Front respect life and love animals. I myself have a white rat whom I kiss on the mouth every day.

Jean-Marie Le Pen, right-wing French politician

We want to save the little furry-feathery guy and all of that, but I don't want to see 40,000 loggers thrown out of work.

President George Bush, Sr., on the Endangered Species Act

ANSWERS

I think we're on the road to coming up with answers that I don't think any of us in total feel we have the answers to.

Mayor Kim Anderson of Naples, Florida

I answer in the affirmative with an emphatic, 'No!'

Sir Boyle Roche MP

I am providing you with a copulation of answers to several questions raised.

Mayor Marion Barry of Washington DC, attempting to say 'compilation'

It's white.

President George W. Bush, on being asked by a child what the White House was like

APOLOGIES

I will never apologise for the United States of America – I don't care what the facts are.

President George Bush, Sr.

ARMED FORCES

The only way we'll ever get a volunteer army is to draft them.

Congressman F. Edward Herbert of Louisiana

Marijuana smokers, drug addicts, long-hairs, homosexuals and unionists.

Chilean President Augusto Pinochet, describing the West German army

Part of the great success was the fact we have an all volunteer army, and part of the all – the military. And part of the rationale is people will have more say in what they want to do. So a mother – I want to be part of this. I can respect and understand that.

President George Bush, Sr.

How long is the Minister prepared to hold up the skirts of Wrens for the convenience of His Majesty's sailors?

Dame Irene Ward MP, on delays in providing uniforms for the Women's Royal Naval Service

I do think we need for a troop to be able to house his family. That's an important part of building morale in the military.

President George W. Bush

Their military uniforms were all different –
chiefly green.

Sir Boyle Roche MP

The pale face of the British soldier is the
backbone of our Indian army.

Anon. Scottish MP

Imagine – the European Commission might
want to harmonise uniforms and cap badges,
or even metricate them. The European Court
would probably want to stop our men
fighting for more than forty hours a week.
They would send half of them home on
paternity leave.

**Michael Portillo MP, on the prospects of a
European Defence Force**

ASSISTANCE

They need help, and we have helped, and we
are here to help. And we are helping, and
we're going to continue to help.

Vice President Dan Quayle

The most terrifying words in the English language are, 'I'm from the government and I'm here to help.'

President Ronald Reagan

ASTROLOGY

I've not lived my life by it, but I won't answer the question the other way because I don't know enough about it to say, is there something to it or not.

President Ronald Reagan, upon being asked if he believed in astrology

BANKING

Bank failures are caused by depositors who don't deposit enough money to cover losses due to mismanagement.

Vice President Dan Quayle

BEAUTY

She has eyes like Caligula and the mouth of
Marilyn Monroe.

**French President Francois Mitterrand, on
Margaret Thatcher**

BEGGARS

Most beggars are Scottish and I've never met
one yet who politely and gently asked for
money. There are no genuine beggars. Those
who are in need have got all the social
benefits they require. Beggars are doing so
out of choice because they find it more
pleasant. I always give them something – I
give them a piece of my mind.

David Maclean MP

BELGIUM

Belgium is a country invented by the British
to annoy the French.

French President Charles de Gaulle

BELLIGERENCE

I often think how much easier the world would have been to manage if Herr Hitler and Signor Mussolini had been at Oxford.

**Lord Halifax, Foreign Secretary
from 1938 until 1941**

BRIBERY

Bribe expenses are tax deductible, provided companies can document that they were necessary to secure a sale of goods or a business contract.

Ole Stavad, Danish tax minister

The idea that a congressman would be tainted by accepting money from private industry or private sources is essentially a socialist argument.

**Newt Gingrich, Speaker of the House of
Representatives**

Don't buy a single vote more than necessary. I'll be damned if I'm going to pay for a landslide.

President John F. Kennedy

BUDGETS

We spend weeks and hours every day
preparing the budget.

President Ronald Reagan

It's clearly a budget. It's got a lot of numbers
in it.

President George W. Bush

I am not worried about the deficit. It is big
enough to take care of itself.

President Ronald Reagan

My plan plays down an unprecedented
amount of our national debt.

**President George W. Bush, commenting
on his first budget**

BUSINESS

I understand small business growth. I was
one.

President George W. Bush

Businessmen should stand or fall on their own two feet.

Edwina Currie MP

CAMPAIGNING

Well, that's going to be up to the pundits and the people to make up their mind. I'll tell you what is a President for him, for example, talking about my record in the state of Texas. I mean, he's willing to say anything in order to convince people that I haven't had a good record in Texas.

President George W. Bush

Michael Heseltine canvassed like a child molester hanging around the lavatories.

Norman Lamont MP

Richard Nixon has been sitting in the White House while George McGovern has been exposing himself to the people of the United States.

Governor Frank Licht of Rhode Island, on the US presidential race

Harold Wilson has been going around the country stirring up apathy.

William Whitelaw MP

Wherever I have gone in this country, I have found Americans.

Alf Landon, touring America whilst campaigning against F. D. Roosevelt

The fact that we can be in two places at once is a good advantage.

David Steel MP, on his and David Owen's 1987 election campaign

I'm not going to focus on what I have done in the past, what I stand for, what I articulate to the American people. The American people will judge me on what I'm saying and what I have done in the last twelve years in Congress.

Dan Quayle

If you're sick and tired of the politics of cynicism and polls and principles, come and join this campaign.

George W. Bush, during a presidential campaign speech

CANADA

We don't come here for our health. We can think of other ways of enjoying ourselves.

Prince Philip, whilst in Canada

CAPITAL PUNISHMENT

Capital punishment is our society's recognition of the sanctity of human life.

Senator Orrin Hatch of Utah

I'm for a stronger death penalty.

President George Bush, Sr.

I'm pro-death. I believe in the death penalty. Let's get on with it.

Mayor Richard M. Daley of Chicago

Life is indeed precious, and I believe the death penalty helps to affirm this fact.

Mayor Ed Koch of New York

I favour capital punishment. It saves lives.

First Lady Nancy Reagan

Those of us who have spent some time in the agricultural sector and in the heartland understand how unfair the death penalty is. Er, the death tax. It's unfair. We've got to get rid of it.

President George W. Bush

Only a governor can make executions happen. I did. And I will.

Governor Mark White of Texas, campaigning for re-election in 1990

Where would Christianity be if Jesus had got eight to fifteen years with time off for good behaviour?

Senator James Donovan of New York

CAREERS

I went up the greasy pole of politics step by step.

Michael Heseltine MP

You know, I would rather have been a professional golfer, but my family pushed me into politics.

Vice President Dan Quayle

Politics is not a bad profession. If you succeed there are many rewards, and if you disgrace yourself you can always write a book.

President Ronald Reagan

Norman Lamont knows his political future is behind him.

Tony Banks MP

CAYMAN ISLANDS

Aren't most of you descended from pirates?

Prince Philip, speaking to a Cayman Islander

CENSORSHIP

Without censorship, things can get terribly confused in the public mind.

General William Westmoreland

CHANGE

This is the advent of a new beginning of continued change.

President Ronald Reagan

Whatever happens will be for the worse, and therefore it is in our interest that as little as possible should happen.

Lord Salisbury

CHANNEL TUNNEL

The cost of the Eurotunnel project has risen, but it is usual in these projects and the Anglo-French consortium is looking into ways to bridge the gap.

Cecil Parkinson MP

CHILDREN

My seven year old, who is now ten ...

Lady Olga Maitland MP

Laura and I really don't realise how bright our children is sometimes until we get an objective analysis.

President George W. Bush

Little children who could neither walk nor talk were running about in the streets cursing their Maker.

Sir Boyle Roche MP

We have become a grandmother.

Margaret Thatcher, Prime Minister

When Mrs Thatcher said, 'We are a grandmother,' she was including Denis in her remarks.

Lord Prior

CHINA

If you stay here much longer you'll all be slitty-eyed.

Prince Philip, speaking to British students in China

China is a big country, inhabited by many Chinese.

French President Charles de Gaulle

If it has got four legs and it is not a chair, if it has got two wings and it flies but it is not an aeroplane, and if it swims and it is not a submarine, the Cantonese will eat it.

Prince Philip

They'll turn it into hors d'oeuvres for Deng Xiaoping, who, I'm told, eats four puppies a day.

Gareth Evans, Australian Foreign Minister, on Hong Kong governor Chris Patten's missing dog

CHOICES

The senator has got to understand if he's going to have – he can't have it both ways. He can't take the high horse and then claim the low road.

President George W. Bush on Senator John McCain

It's a question of whether we're going forward into the future, or past to the back.

Vice President Dan Quayle

CLONING

It would be a mistake for the United States Senate to allow any kind of human cloning to come out of that chamber.

President George W. Bush

COLLEAGUES

Gerald Ford was a Communist.

President Ronald Reagan, attempting to say 'congressman'

I have probably known Michael Heseltine longer than anyone else for the last sixteen years.

Chairman of the Henley-on-Thames Conservative Association

For seven and a half years, I've worked
alongside President Reagan. We've had some
triumphs. Made some mistakes. We've had
some sex.

**President George Bush, Sr., attempting
to say 'setbacks'**

They asked me to go in front of the Reagans.
I'm not used to going in front of President
Reagan, so I went out behind the Bushes.

Vice President Dan Quayle

COMMUNICATION

We're sending 23 million leaflets to every
household in Britain.

Norman Fowler MP

Two things are absolutely clear, and I want
to make them absolutely clear.

Harriet Harman MP

He can talk over the heads of the
intelligentsia to the grass roots level.

John Brown MP

We offer the party as a big tent. How we do that within the platform, the preamble to the platform, or whatnot, that remains to be seen. But that message will have to be articulated with great clarity.

Vice President Dan Quayle

I think I've got to do better in making clear what the message is, and I think I can do better. But I think there's so much noise out there that I've got to figure out how to make it clearer that we are for the things that I have advocated that would help.

President George Bush, Sr.

I don't want to make any previous statement on that.

George Schultz, US Secretary of State

While I write this letter, I have a pistol in one hand and a sword in the other.

Sir Boyle Roche MP

But that I'm out of touch with the American people, that I don't know people are hurting, I know it. I feel it. We pray about it, and I mean that literally at night, and – er – many things, the various, where I don't care about, don't know about education or don't, I mean,

we've got a sound approach, innovative,
revolutionary approach, and so I have to
make that clear.

President George Bush, Sr.

The light which the Lord Chancellor had
thrown upon the matter was darkness.

Lord Ribblesdale

No comment, but don't quote me.

Vice President Dan Quayle

I should have answered your letter a
fortnight ago, but I only received it this
morning.

Sir Boyle Roche MP

COMPLAINTS

They pushed their nomination down my
throat behind my back.

J. Ramsey MacDonald, Prime Minister

It's the most unheard-of thing I've ever
heard of.

Senator Joseph McCarthy

They're stretching belief beyond all possible credulity.

Neil Kinnock MP

It's like an Alcatraz around my neck.

Mayor Menino of Boston

They blew the talks out of the water before they even got off the ground.

Jimmy Knapp, leader of the Railwaymen's Union

I told you to make one longer than another, and instead you have made one shorter than the other, the opposite.

Sir Boyle Roche MP

I'm not going to have some reporters pawing through our papers. We are the President.

First Lady Hillary Clinton, commenting on the release of subpoenaed documents

Gentlemen, a member of this House has taken advantage of my absence to tweak my nose behind my back. I hope that the next time he abuses me behind my back like a coward he will do it to my face like a man, and not go skulking into the thicket to assail a gentleman who isn't present to defend himself.

Anon. Australian MP

COMPROMISE

I hear the stench of appeasement.

Margaret Thatcher, Prime Minister

Bridge-building is a one-way street.

Jonathan Aitken MP

CONSERVATIVES

If capitalism depended on the intellectual quality of the Conservative Party, it would end about lunchtime tomorrow.

Tony Benn MP

Conservatism is the political equivalent of bed-wetting.

Hywel Williams MP

Many Americans don't like the simple things. That's what they have against us conservatives.

**Republican presidential candidate
Barry Goldwater**

A Conservative government is an organised hypocrisy.

**Benjamin Disraeli, Conservative Prime
Minister**

The Conservative Party in the House of Commons contains the party conference of ten years ago. Cheerful girls in hats who once moved motions in favour of corporal and capital punishment on behalf of the Young Conservatives of some Midlands town, small-town solicitors and estate agents with flat provincial accents are now its members. As Mrs Thatcher went up in the world, so the Party came down.

**Sir Julian Critchley MP, Conservative
politician**

CONSTITUTIONAL ISSUES

If this were a dictatorship, it would be a heck of a lot easier so long as I'm the dictator.

President George W. Bush

The illegal we do immediately. The unconstitutional takes a little longer.

Henry Kissinger, US Secretary of State

What right does Congress have to go around making laws just because they deem it necessary?

Mayor Marion Barry of Washington DC

I support efforts to limit the terms of members of Congress, especially members of the House and members of the Senate.

Vice President Dan Quayle

I am mindful of the difference between the executive branch and the legislative branch. I assured all four of these leaders that I know the difference, and the difference is they pass the laws and I execute them.

President George W. Bush

The theories, the ideas she expressed about
equality of results within legislative bodies
and with – by outcome, by decisions made
by legislative bodies, ideas related to
proportional voting as a general remedy, not
in particular cases where circumstances
make that a feasible idea.

Vice President Al Gore

I am mindful not only of preserving
executive powers for myself, but for my
predecessors as well.

President George W. Bush

The legislature's job is to write law. It's the
executive branch's job to interpret law.

President George W. Bush

There are lots more people in the House. I
don't know exactly – I've never counted, but
at least a couple hundred.

**Vice President Dan Quayle, commenting on
the difference between the House and Senate**

CONTENTMENT

You all look like happy campers to me. Happy campers you are, happy campers you have been, and, as far as I am concerned, happy campers you will always be.

Vice President Dan Quayle

CRIME

There are more crimes in Britain now, due to a huge rise in the crime rate.

Neil Kinnock MP

Interviewer: How do you explain this rise in crime?

Douglas Hurd MP: There's so much more to nick.

When the President does it, that means it's not illegal.

President Richard Nixon

If people had proper locks on their doors, crime could be prevented before it happens.

Douglas Hurd MP

The more killing and homicides you have,
the more havoc it prevents.

Mayor Richard J. Daley of Chicago

I believe in preventing unnecessary crime.

**Angela Rumbold, Conservative candidate for
Mitcham and Morden, in 1997**

The police are fully able to meet and compete
with the criminals.

Mayor John F. Hylan of New York

Outside the killings, Washington has one of
the lowest crime rates in the country.

Mayor Marion Barry of Washington DC

If crime went down one hundred per cent, it
would still be fifty times higher than it
should be.

John Bowman, Washington DC Councilman

I haven't committed a crime. What I did was
fail to comply with the law.

Mayor David Dinkins of New York

I was on federal probation for shooting up
mailboxes. I got into a fistfight. I was locked
up for disturbing the peace. I was twenty

years old. What the hell does that have to do with Al Simpson at fifty-seven? What is this crap?

Senator Alan Simpson of Wyoming

CRISES

This is anarchy gone mad.

Anon. Union Official

There cannot be a world crisis next week. My schedule is full.

Henry Kissinger, US Secretary of State

This is the worst disaster in California since I was elected.

Governor Pat Brown of California, commenting on local floods

The cup of our trouble is running over, but, alas, is not yet full.

Sir Boyle Roche MP

Here we have a government disintegrating between our eyes.

John Prescott MP

I have orders to be awakened at any time in case of a national emergency, even if I'm in a cabinet meeting.

President Ronald Reagan

There's no question that the minute I got elected, the storm clouds on the horizon were getting nearly directly overhead.

President George W. Bush

I concluded from the beginning that this would be the end, and I am right, for it is not half over yet.

Sir Boyle Roche MP

CRITICISM

It's a typical example of this government saying one thing with one hand and another thing with the other hand.

Rob Greg, at the Liberal Democrats' Party Conference

The Unionist Parliament was without spine or backbone.

Reverend Ian Paisley MP

President Carter speaks loudly and carries a fly spotter, a fly swasher. It's been a long day.

President Gerald Ford

CRITICS

Even though there may be some misguided critics of what we're trying to do, I think we're on the wrong path.

President Ronald Reagan

They misunderestimated me.

President George W. Bush

Some reporters said I don't have any vision. Well, I don't see that.

President George Bush, Sr.

DEBATE

Nothing happened until I pressed the minister on the floor of the house.

David Alton MP

DECISION-MAKING

I can assure you that I definitely might take action.

Lord Whitelaw

I'm not indecisive. Am I indecisive?

Mayor Jim Scheibel of St. Paul, Minnesota

Interviewer: Which word best sums up your character?

Paddy Ashdown MP: Er – perhaps 'decisive'?

We don't believe in planners and deciders making the decisions on behalf of Americans.

President George W. Bush

I can assure you that I definitely might take action.

William Whitelaw MP

As I've said before and I said yesterday, this is one of the key questions that will be decided or not decided at Edinburgh.

Douglas Hurd MP

I have made good judgements in the past. I have made good judgements in the future.

President George Bush, Sr.

This administration is doing everything we can to end the stalemate in an efficient way. We're making the right decisions to bring the solution to an end.

President George W. Bush

There is always a choice of whether one does it last week, this week, or next week.

John Major, Prime Minister

DEFEAT

At the end of the day, isn't it time we called it a day?

John Morris MP

DEFENCE POLICY

We cannot let terrorists and rogue nations hold this nation hostile or hold our allies hostile.

President George W. Bush

Why wouldn't an enhanced deterrent, a
more stable peace, a better prospect of
denying the ones who enter conflict in the
first place to have a reduction of offensive
systems and an introduction to defensive
capability. I believe that is the route this
country will eventually go.

Vice President Dan Quayle

But the true threats to stability and peace are
these nations that are not very transparent,
that hide behind the – that don't let people
in to take a look and see what they're up to.
They're very kind of authoritarian regimes.
The true threat is whether or not one of
these people decide, peak of anger, try to
hold us hostage, ourselves; the Israelis, for
example, to whom we'll defend, offer our
defences; the South Koreans.

President George W. Bush

Russia is no longer our enemy and therefore
we shouldn't be locked into a Cold War
mentality that says we keep the peace by
blowing each other up. In my attitude, that's
old, that's tired, that's stale.

President George W. Bush

DEMOCRACY

All of these black people are screwing up my democracy.

Ian Smith, Rhodesian Prime Minister

Democracy is more important than having a parliament.

Dr Peter Onu, Assistant Secretary General of the Organisation of African Unity

I can't believe that we're going to let a majority of people decide what is best for this state.

Louisiana Representative John Travis

We're the most democratic country in Latin America.

Fidel Castro, Cuban leader

I intend to open the country up to democracy, and anyone who is against that I will jail, I will crush.

Brazilian President Joao Figueiredo

DISABILITY

My, you must have fun chasing the soap around the bath!

Princess Diana, upon meeting a one-armed man

Do you know they now do eating dogs for anorexics?

Prince Philip to a blind woman with a guide dog

DISARMAMENT

Our security and our hopes for success at the arms reduction talks hinge on the determination that we show to continue our programme to rebuild and refortify our defences.

President Ronald Reagan

I see no media mention of it, but we entered in – you asked me what the time is and I'm telling you how to build a watch here – but we had Boris Yeltsin here the other day. And I think of my times campaigning in Iowa, years ago, and how there was a – Iowa has a kind of, I single out Iowa, it's kind of an international state in a sense and has a great interest in all these things – and we had Yeltsin standing here in the Rose Garden, and we entered into a deal to eliminate the biggest and most threatening ballistic missiles. And it was almost, 'Ho-hum, what have you done for me lately?'

President George Bush, Sr.

DISCRIMINATION

One important new area is proposed legislation to promote unfair discrimination against people with disabilities.

Cabinet Office's Forward Look of Government-funded Science, Engineering and Technology, 1995

That's part of American greatness – discrimination. Yes sir, inequality breeds freedom and gives a man opportunity.

Governor Lester Maddox of Georgia

I stand for anti-bigotry, anti-Semitism, anti-racism. That is what drives me.

President George Bush, Sr.

Because she's a damn lesbian. I'm not going to put a lesbian in a position like that. If you want to call me a bigot, fine.

Senator Jesse Helms, on his attempt to block the appointment of Roberta Achtenberg as Assistant Secretary of Housing and Urban Development

Unfairly, but truthfully, our party has been tagged as being against things. Anti-immigrant, for example.

President George W. Bush

DISCUSSION

An extraordinary affair. I gave them their orders and they wanted to stay and discuss them.

Duke of Wellington, describing his first Cabinet meeting as Prime Minister

Actually, I – this may sound a little West Texan to you, but I like it – when I'm talking about – when I'm talking about myself, and when he's talking about myself, all of us are talking about me.

President George W. Bush

DIVERSITY

We have every kind of mixture you can have.
I have a black, I have a woman, two Jews
and a cripple.

James Watt, US Interior Secretary in 1983

DOCTORS

It is surprising that the present bitter
controversy has arisen between the
Government and, on the one hand, the
Labour Party – and to some extent the centre
parties as well – and, on the other, the
British Medical Opposition – British Medical
Association. That is certainly my most
Freudian slip of the tongue so far.

Kenneth Clarke MP

Certain elements of the British Medical
Association leadership have gone over the
top and taken fully entrenched positions.

Nicholas Winterton MP

DRUGS

Now, like, I'm President. It would be pretty hard for some drug guy to come into the White House and start offering it up, you know? I bet if they did, I hope I would say, 'Hey, get lost. We don't want any of that.'

President George Bush, Sr.

Interviewer: What should you do if your children want to talk about solvent abuse?

Brian Mawhinney MP: Take a deep breath ...

Interviewer: Why do so many Americans use illicit drugs?

George Bush, Sr.: Yeah, well I think there's some social change going on. AIDS, for example, is – er – is – er – is a – er – a disease of poverty in a sense. It's where the hopelessness is. It's bigger than that, of course.

When I was in England, I experimented with marijuana a time or two, and I didn't like it, and I didn't inhale, and I never tried it again.

President Bill Clinton

I never did drugs. That's the only thing I missed out on. I never smoked – what do you call that ol' thing? Shit.

Charlie McCreevy, Irish Minister for Finance

I don't – sorry – I do not – the moment you ask me that question you immediately have the right to ask anyone that question and I do not accept the validity of the question.

Paddy Ashdown MP, upon being asked if he had ever taken drugs

ECONOMIC POLICY

I'm concerned about the Japanese devaluation issue.

President George W. Bush on the Japanese deflation issue. His mistake caused a rush to sell the Yen on the international money markets

The growth of post-neo-classical endogenous growth theory and the symbiotic relationships between growth and investment.

Gordon Brown MP

We must prosper America first.

President Warren Harding

It is a tricky problem to find the particular calibration in timing that would be appropriate to stem the acceleration in risk premiums created by falling incomes without prematurely aborting the decline in the inflation-generated risk premiums.

Alan Greenspan, Chairman of the Federal Reserve

I mean, these good folks are revolutionising how businesses conduct their business. And, like them, I am very optimistic about our position in the world and its influence on the United States. We're concerned about the short-term economic news, but long-term I'm optimistic. And so, I hope investors, you know – secondly, I hope investors hold investments for periods of time – that I've always found the best investments are those that you salt away based on economics.

President George W. Bush

To the extent that when one measures real interest rates by effectively subtracting the inflation rate from the nominal interest rates, if there is a bias in the inflation rate, and it hasn't changed very significantly, it means that the level of inflation that – once it subtracts from the nominal interest rate – is lower across the board of history, and that the real interest rate measured is correspondingly higher.

Alan Greenspan, Chairman of the Federal Reserve

Ronald Reagan has done for monetarism what the Boston strangler did for door-to-door salesmen.

Denis Healey MP

A billion here, a billion there and pretty soon you're talking about real money.

Senator Everett Dirksen

Sustainable growth is growth that is sustainable.

John Major, Prime Minister

These cornerstones were the centre of the Chancellor's policy.

Gordon Brown MP

Both economically, politically and socially ...

Neil Kinnock MP

It was always my opinion, when working at the Ministry of Defence, that those at the Treasury worked for the Russians. Nothing has since persuaded me that I am wrong.

Nicholas Soames MP

ECONOMY

If I listened to Michael Dukakis long enough I would be convinced that we're in an economic downturn and people are homeless and going without food and medical attention and that we've got to do something about the unemployed.

President Ronald Reagan

Blessed are the young, for they shall inherit the national debt.

President Herbert Hoover

Working mothers are the backbone of the third half of the economy.

Glenda Jackson MP

We took the kettle off the boil and overheated the economy.

Geoffrey Dickens MP

The condition of the country wasn't handed down in tablets of stone from Mount Olympus.

Margaret Beckett MP

EDUCATION

We have to understand that standards vary far too great between schools.

Estelle Morris MP, Secretary of State for Education

One of the great things about books is sometimes there are some fantastic pictures.

President George W. Bush

Headmasters of schools tend to be men.

Clare Short MP

We will not be abolishing the right to buy schooling – it's just that parents will have to buy it abroad.

Neil Kinnock MP

At the end of the day in the morning there's not much else a teacher can do if the child doesn't turn up for school.

Estelle Morris MP

If any of you have got an A-level, it is because you have worked to get it. Go to any other country and when you have got an A-level, you have bought it.

Michael Portillo MP

Interviewer: How will you make a difference as 'the education President'?

George Bush, Sr.: You'll be able to send your college to children.

We're going to have the best-educated Americans in the world.

Vice President Dan Quayle

It is time to set aside the old partisan bickering and finger-pointing and name-calling that comes from freeing parents to make different choices for their children.

President George W. Bush

I want it to be said that the Bush administration was a results-oriented administration, because I believe the results of focussing our attention and energy on teaching children to read and having an education system that's responsive to the child and to the parents, as opposed to mired in a system that refuses to change, will make America what we want it to be – a more literate country and a hopefuller country.

President George W. Bush

That's fine phonetically, but you're missing just a little bit.

Vice President Dan Quayle, adding an 'e' to 'potato'

You can now get a certificate to teach German by sitting through enough classes, but if you speak German, you can't teach German if you don't have a certificate. So you can have a German teacher who can't speak German, but though they have the certificate so they can teach, even though they can't teach. If you can speak it, you can't teach it, even if you could teach it. Are you with me so far?

Newt Gingrich, Speaker of the House of Representatives

And let me say in conclusion, thanks to the kids. I learned an awful lot about bathtub toys – about how to work the telephone. One guy knows – several of them know their own phone numbers – preparation to go to the dentist. A lot of things I'd forgotten. So it's been a good day.

President George Bush, Sr., after visiting a school

You teach a child to read, and he or her will be able to pass a literacy test.

President George W. Bush

Reading is the basics for all learning.

President George W. Bush

Burnham Category II/III courses may or may not be advanced and poolable. A Burnham Category II/III course which is not poolable is not poolable only because it is not advanced, i.e. it does not require course approval as an advanced course. It is therefore wrong to ascribe it as a 'non-poolable advanced (non-designated) course'. Non-poolable courses are non-advanced by definition. I think that the problem you have described probably results from confusion here.

Lord Elwyn Jones, quoting from a letter from the Department of Education

Rarely is the question asked: is our children learning?

President George W. Bush

Quite frankly, teachers are the only profession that teaches our children.

Vice President Dan Quayle

ELECTIONS

The Fermanagh by-election is not about the IRA hunger strikes, but about bread-and-butter issues.

Eamonn Malley

If you would know the depth of meanness of human nature, you have got to be a Prime Minister running a general election.

John A. Macdonald, Canadian Prime Minister

I wouldn't be seen dead saying that the Conservatives would win the next election.

David Blunkett MP

All I was doing was appealing for an endorsement, not suggesting you endorse it.

President George Bush, Sr.

The only way that the Republican Party can hold the White House is to nominate a candidate who can win.

Alexander Haig, US Secretary of State

If elected, I will win.

Pat Paulsen, US presidential candidate

I knew it might put him in an awkward position that we had a discussion before finality has finally happened in this presidential race.

President George W. Bush

As far as the legal hassling and wrangling and posturing in Florida, I would suggest you talk to our team in Florida led by Jim Baker.

President George W. Bush

As the Reagan presidency ends, it is time for the Bush pregnancy to begin.

Governor Tommy Thompson of Wisconsin

ELECTRICITY

The California crunch really is the result of not enough power-generating plants and then not enough power to power the power of generating plants.

President George W. Bush

EMPLOYMENT RELATIONS

The interests of the employers and the employed are the same nine times out of ten. I will even say ninety-nine times out of ten.

Lord Curzon

ENTHUSIASM

Immediately every man in the place, including women and children, ran out to meet them.

Sir Boyle Roche MP

ENVIRONMENTAL ISSUES

Anyway, I'm so thankful, and so gracious –
I'm gracious that my brother Jeb is
concerned about the hemisphere as well.

President George W. Bush

The American Petroleum Institute filed suit
against the Environmental Protection Agency
and charged that the agency was
suppressing a scientific study for fear it
might be misinterpreted. The suppressed
study reveals that eighty per cent of air
pollution comes not from chimneys and auto
exhaust pipes, but from plants and trees.

President Ronald Reagan

It is exciting to have a real crisis like the
Falklands on your hands when you have
spent half your political life dealing with
humdrum issues like the environment.

Margaret Thatcher, Prime Minister

There's been a lot made of this dirty man of
Europe business, but I don't think it washes.

**Tom Burke, special adviser at the
Department of Environment**

Your country is one of the most notorious centres of trading endangered species in the world.

Prince Philip in Thailand to accept a conservation award

Trees have to be cut down and replanted.

Nicholas Ridley MP

We've got to pause and ask ourselves – how much clean air do we need?

Lee Iococca, Chairman of the Chrysler Corporation

In Ireland we still have one of the best environments in Europe but there have been a number of serious pollution problems to our livers and lakes.

Charles Haughey, Irish Prime Minister

It isn't pollution that's harming our environment. It's the impurities in our air and water that are doing it.

Vice President Dan Quayle

Approximately eighty per cent of our air pollution stems from hydrocarbons released by vegetation.

President Ronald Reagan

First, we would not accept a treaty that would not have been ratified, nor a treaty that I thought made sense for the country.

President George W. Bush, commenting on the Kyoto Treaty

There are some monuments where the land is so widespread, they just encompass as much as possible. And the integral part of the – the precious part, so to speak – I guess all land is precious, but the part that the people uniformly would not want to spoil, will not be despoiled. But there are parts of the monument lands where we can explore without affecting the overall environment.

President George W. Bush

I am wearing a dinosaur tie today, and I did it deliberately. And it occurred to me – I want to make two points about this dinosaur tie. This is a – I think a tyrannosaurus – I mean a triceratops – coming out of the egg. The first point I want to make is that they're extinct and that you could take that as a sort of warning to us that these things happen. The second point I want to make is that they're extinct, and that in fact life is like that. I think on the one hand when people say, you know, let's preserve X, well, my first point is going to be if at some point in the next 50,000 years the Earth tilts, as it will – at least it has

63

now so far for its entire history – that slight tilt will change totally the ecosystem you're prepared currently to spend endless quantities to save. At that point the Sahara may well once again bloom as it used to and you may have new deserts in areas that are now wet, and that's in fact the nature of history over time. Now, I'd love to see what a troglodyte would be like if it were alive, but I'm not sure that in and of itself that ought to be the end point. Are people a part of the ecosystem or are people in fact aliens?

Newt Gingrich, Speaker of the House of Representatives

You can't just let nature run wild.

Governor Walter Hickel of Alaska

A tree's a tree. How many do you need to look at?

President Ronald Reagan

The best thing about rain forests is that they never suffer from any drought.

Vice President Dan Quayle

The green belt is a Labour achievement and we mean to build on it.

John Prescott MP

If the environmentalists had their way, we'd all be living in rabbits' holes and birds' nests.

President Ronald Reagan

EQUALITY

We need more inequality in order to eliminate poverty.

Sir Keith Joseph

My goal is an America where something or anything that is done to or for anyone is done neither because of nor in spite of any differences between them racially, religiously or ethnic origin-wise.

President Ronald Reagan

ETHICS

It's a devastating issue if you're on the wrong side of it.

Newt Gingrich, Speaker of the House of Representatives, on ethics

EUROPE

All those people who say there will never be a single European currency are trying to forecast history.

Kenneth Clarke MP

We're members of the European Union now. If you're a Portuguese window-cleaner, you can now come and clean windows in London. If you're a Portuguese footballer, ditto.

David Mellor MP

If we enter it, in two years time there will not be a snail on our walls, a frog in our ponds, or a fish in our bays.

Joe Lenehan, Irish politician, on the Common Market

We'll negotiate a withdrawal from the EEC which has drained our natural resources and destroyed jobs.

Tony Blair, before he became an MP, in 1983

The Maastricht Treaty has been dealt, at least temporarily, a fatal blow.

Des O'Malley, Irish politician

Attempts to make Europe right and pure by being nice to those who want to divide it in their own interests won't work. All being called Schmidt and speaking Esperanto is not the way ahead.

Sir Nicholas Fairbairn MP

It's a German racket to take over the whole of Europe. It has to be thwarted.

Nicholas Ridley MP, on European monetary union

If Europe stays still it will start going backwards.

Paddy Ashdown MP

EXCUSES

I didn't accept it. I received it.

Richard Allen, National Security Adviser to President Ronald Reagan, explaining the $1,000 in cash and two watches he was given by Japanese journalists

A man could not be in two places at the same time unless he were a bird.

Sir Boyle Roche MP

EXPECTATIONS

One of the common denominators I have found is that expectations rise above that which is expected.

President George W. Bush

EXPERIMENTS

The idea of a pilot scheme is to see whether it will fly.

Lord Young

FACTS

And if I could just correct one fact ...

John Prescott MP

The fact that he relies on facts – says things that are not factual – are going to undermine his campaign.

President George W. Bush on Al Gore

The single, overwhelming two facts are ...

Paddy Ashdown MP

Facts are stupid things.

President Ronald Reagan

FAMILY

I mean, a child that doesn't have a parent to read to that child or that doesn't see that when the child is hurting to have a parent and help out or neither parent there enough to pick the kid up and dust him off and send him back into the game at school or whatever, that kid has a disadvantage.

President George Bush, Sr.

I believe in the natural family order where the man works and the woman stays at home and raises the kids. It's what the people want and what they will get if I am elected.

Larry Forgy, Republican candidate for governor of Kentucky, 1991

Don't forget about the importance of the family. It begins with the family. We're not going to redefine the family. Everybody knows the definition of the family. A child. A mother. A father. There are other arrangements of the family, but that is a family and family values. I've been very blessed with wonderful parents and a wonderful family, and I am proud of my family. Anybody turns to their family. I have a very good family. I'm very fortunate to have a very good family. I believe strongly in family. It's one of the things we have in our platform, is to talk about it. I suppose three important things certainly come to my mind that we want to say thank you. The first would be our family. Your family, my family – which is composed of an immediate family of a wife and three children, a larger family with grandparents and aunts and uncles. We all have our family, whichever that may be. The very beginnings of civilisation, the very beginnings of this country, goes back to the family. And time and time again, I'm often reminded, especially in this presidential campaign, of the importance of family, and what a family means to this country. And so when you pay thanks I suppose the first thing that would come to mind would be to thank the Lord for the family.

Vice President Dan Quayle

It is in everyone's interests to reduce broken families and the number of single parents. I have seen from my own constituency the consequences of marital breakdown.

Tim Yeo MP, shortly before the revelations about his mistress and illegitimate child became public

It's important to allay the finger of responsibility at the door of parents.

John Patten MP

Families is where our nation finds hope, where wings take dream.

President George W. Bush

We live in a world where the Kelloggs Cornflake family is ever less rare.

Virginia Bottomley MP

FAMINE

Nobody who has seen the pictures can be remotely other than greatly concerned.

Douglas Hurd MP

FARMING

Interviewer: How do target prices actually work?

Dan Quayle: Target prices? How that works? I know quite a bit about farm policy. I come from Indiana, which is a farm state. Deficiency payments, which are the key – that is what gets money into the farmers' hands. We've got loan – er – rates. We've got target – er –prices – erm – I have worked very closely with my senior colleague, Richard Lugar, making sure that the farmers of Indiana are taken care of.

FIELD SPORTS

The grouse are in no danger from those who shoot grouse.

Prince Philip

FISHING

If this country ever loses its interest in fishing, we got real trouble.

President George Bush, Sr.

FOOD

I never see any home cooking – all I get is fancy stuff.

Prince Philip

You can slice me up, but that won't last you for long.

Russian President Boris Yeltsin, upon being asked what the people should eat during food shortages

Nobody need be worried about BSE in this country or anywhere else.

John Gummer MP, Agriculture Minister, in 1990

If people wish to eat meat and run the risk of dying a horrible, lingering, hormone-induced death after sprouting extra breasts and large amounts of hair it is, of course, entirely up to them.

Tony Banks MP

It's difficult to believe people are still starving in this country because food isn't available.

President Ronald Reagan

I know how hard it is for you to put food on your family.

President George W. Bush

I was dramatically shaped by my grandmother and my aunts because they convinced me there was always a cookie available. Deep down inside me I'm four years old, and I wake up and I think out there, there's a cookie. Every morning I'm going, you know, either it can be baked or it's already been bought, but it's in a jar. Somewhere. And so that means when you open up the cupboard and the cookie isn't there, I don't say, 'Gee, there's no cookie.' I say, 'I wonder where it is?'

Newt Gingrich, Speaker of the House of Representatives

British women can't cook.

Prince Philip

FOREIGN POLICY

This foreign policy stuff is a little frustrating.

President George W. Bush

George Bush has met more heads of foreign states than I have. But a substantial number of them were dead.

Jesse Jackson, US religious leader

I don't do foreign policy.

Newt Gingrich, Speaker of the House of Representatives

He was very forward leaning, as they say in diplomatic nuanced circles.

President George W. Bush

This will mean a sea change in Atlantic relationships.

Henry Kissinger, US Secretary of State

I will have a foreign-handed foreign policy.

President George W. Bush

We have a firm commitment to NATO. We are part of NATO. We have a firm commitment to Europe. We are part of Europe.

Vice President Dan Quayle

We'll let our friends be peacekeepers and the great country called America will be the pace-makers.

President George W. Bush

Keep good relations with the Grecians.

President George W. Bush

Redefining the role of the United States from enablers to keep the peace to enablers to keep the peace from the peacekeepers is going to be an assignment.

President George W. Bush

United Nations' goodwill may be a bottomless pit, but it's by no means limitless.

John Major, Prime Minister

I have said that the sanctions regime is like Swiss cheese – that meant that they weren't very effective.

President George W. Bush

The fundamental question is, 'Will I be a successful President when it comes to foreign policy?' I will be, but until I'm the President it's going to be hard for me to verify that I think I'll be more effective.

President George W. Bush

The two super-powers cannot divide the world into their oyster.

Michael Heseltine MP

FREE SPEECH

You know the one thing that's wrong with this country? Everyone gets a chance to have their fair say.

President Bill Clinton

FREEDOM

It is true that liberty is precious – so precious that it must be rationed.

Lenin

Ours is a great state, and we don't like limits of any kind. Ricky Clunn is one of the great bass fishermen. He's a Texas young guy, and he's a very competitive fisherman, and he talked about learning to fish wading in the creeks behind his dad. He in his underwear went wading in the creeks behind his father, and he said – as a fisherman it's great to grow up in a community with no limits.

President George Bush, Sr.

The truth is that men are tired of liberty.

Benito Mussolini

FUTURE

The future, where most of us are destined to spend the rest of our lives ...

Geoffrey Howe MP

America's future is still ahead of us.

Governor Thomas E. Dewey of New York

Along the untrodden paths of the future, I can see the footprints of an unseen hand.

Sir Boyle Roche MP

Clearly, the future is still to come.

Peter Brooke MP

Things happen more frequently in the future than they do in the past.

Governor Booth Gardner of Washington

It's not the future I'm talking about, I'm talking about tomorrow ...

John Gummer MP

The future is not what it used to be.

Malcolm Rifkind MP

GAS

Natural gas is hemispheric. I like to call it hemispheric in nature because it's a product that we can find in our neighbourhoods.

President George W. Bush

GENDER

Let me tell you, this gender thing is history. You're looking at a guy who sat down with Margaret Thatcher across the table and talked about serious issues.

President George Bush, Sr.

Dennis Skinner MP: How many civil servants in employment at the latest date are (a.) men or (b.) women?

Tim Renton MP: All of them.

GEOGRAPHY

I read about foreign policy and studied – I
know the number of continents.

George Wallace, presidential candidate, 1968

I ask you to join me in a toast to President
Figueiredo and the people of Bolivia – no,
that's where I'm going.

President Ronald Reagan, in Brazil

Carter apparently doesn't even know that
Michigan is one of the forty-eight states.
Fifty. Fifty states. I voted for Hawaii and
Alaska and I'm proud of it.

Former President Gerald Ford, 1980

Tourists go home with the photographs
showing them with one foot in the northern
hemisphere and one in the southern.

Rosie Barnes MP, on Greenwich, London

It is wonderful to be here in the great state
of Chicago.

Vice President Dan Quayle

Is the West Bank a publicly or a privately
owned institution?

Enzo Scotti, Italian Foreign Minister

The only thing I know about Slovakia is what I just learned first-hand from your foreign minister.

President George W. Bush, speaking to a Slovak journalist shortly after a meeting with the Prime Minister of Slovenia

You are a worthy representative of the new democracy in Brazil.

James Callaghan, Prime Minister, toasting the President of Portugal

The Foreign Relations Committee has had the honour of welcoming the distinguished Prime Minister of India.

Senator Jesse Helms, introducing the Pakistani Prime Minister Benazir Bhutto to the Senate

To his majesty the King of Sweden!

James Callaghan MP, proposing a toast to the King of Norway

Tell me, how dead is the Dead Sea?

President George Bush, Sr., during a visit to Jordan

It's marvellous to be in South Island.

The Duke of Devonshire, on arrival in North Island, New Zealand

To the great people and government of Israel – excuse me, of Egypt.

President Gerald Ford, at a banquet given by Anwar Sadat

You too have difficulties with unemployment in the United States.

Margaret Thatcher, Prime Minister, in Canada

It's nice to be in Devon again.

Paddy Ashdown MP, in Cornwall

GERMANY

Those who imagine that Germany has swung back to its old imperial temper cannot have any understanding of the character of the change. The idea of a Germany intimidating Europe with a threat that its irresistible army might march across frontiers forms no part in the new vision. They have no longer the desire themselves to invade any other land.

Lloyd George, former Prime Minister, in 1936

War will not come again. We have a more profound impression than any others of the evil that war causes. Germany's problems cannot be settled by war.

Adolf Hitler, in 1934

GOVERNMENT

Government is like a baby – a huge appetite at one end and no sense of responsibility at the other.

President Ronald Reagan

My mission is humanitarian. Therefore, it in no way represents the British government.

Edward Heath, Prime Minister

GRAMMAR

'If' is a very big preposition.

John Major, Prime Minister

The figures for Stage II Literacy and Numeracy tests stood still, faltered, or stuttered, or whatever adjective you want to use.

Estelle Morris MP, Secretary of State for Education

GRATITUDE

My first qualification for mayor of the City of New York is my monumental ingratitude to each and all of you.

Mayor Fiorello LaGuardia of New York

GREAT BRITAIN

We are not wholly an island, *except* geographically.

John Major, Prime Minister

Anyone would think we were living on some island somewhere.

George Walden MP

GUN CONTROL

For every fatal shooting, there were roughly three non-fatal shootings. And, folks, this is unacceptable in America. It's just unacceptable. And we're going to do something about it.

President George W. Bush

There are various groups that think you can ban certain kinds of – certain kinds of guns. And I am not in that mode. I am in the mode of being deeply concerned.

President George Bush, Sr.

There's no evidence that people who use weapons for sport are any more dangerous than people who use golf clubs or tennis racquets or cricket bats. If a cricketer suddenly decided to go into a school and batter a lot of people to death with a cricket bat – which he could do very easily – are you going to ban cricket bats?

Prince Philip, on the Dunblane massacre

Hey listen. I'm a member of the National Rifle Association. You're hurting my feelings, as they say in China.

President George Bush, Sr.

There are sometimes good reasons why young people need, and can benefit from, proper and controlled access to firearms – for example, if they are growing up on a farm.

Ann Widdecombe MP

I come from a state where gun control is just how steady you hold your weapon.

Senator Alan Simpson of Wyoming

HAWAII

Hawaii is a unique state. It is a small state. It is a state that is by itself. It is a – it is different from the other forty-nine states. Well, all states are different, but it's got a particularly unique situation.

Vice President Dan Quayle

Hawaii has always been a very pivotal role in the Pacific. It is in the Pacific. It is part of the United States that is an island that is right there.

Vice President Dan Quayle

HEALTH

Suicide is a real threat to health in a modern society.

Virginia Bottomley MP

Speaking as a man, it's not a woman's issue. Us men are tired of losing our women.

Vice President Dan Quayle, on breast cancer

Drug therapies are replacing a lot of medicines as we used to know it.

President George W. Bush

The Health Service is the flower of our nation and it's crumbling.

Anon. Labour Party spokeman

I think most of the wrinkles have been ironed out.

Teresa Gorman MP, on developments with hormone replacement treatment for older women

People in the north die of ignorance and crisps.

Edwina Currie MP

HISTORY

Who are these people?

Al Gore, looking at busts of George Washington and Benjamin Franklin

History will be kind to me for I intend to write it.

Winston Churchill, Prime Minister

As King Henry VIII said to each of his three wives, 'I won't keep you long'.

President Ronald Reagan

Who is King Billy? Go home, man, and read your Bible.

Reverend Ian Paisley MP

This is the greatest heap of bulldust since Marx first enunciated his Mein Kampf or whatever it was.

Sir Magnus Cormack

That's a chapter, the last chapter of the twentieth – twentieth – the twenty-first century that most of us would rather forget. The last chapter of the twentieth century.

This is the first chapter of the twenty-first century.

President George W. Bush

HOLLAND

What a po-faced lot these Dutch are.

Prince Philip, whilst visiting Amsterdam

HOLOCAUST

The Nazi holocaust was an obscene period in our country's history – well, not our country's history, this century's history. We all lived in this century. I didn't live in this century.

Vice President Dan Quayle

Boy, they were big on crematoriums, weren't they?

President Ronald Reagan, whilst visiting Auschwitz

HOMOSEXUALITY

I believe that people like myself should stand
shoulder to shoulder with the homosexual
fraternity, but you're only likely to get
support if you don't continue to flaunt your
homosexuality and thrust it down other
people's throats.

Geoffrey Dickens MP

I'm not prejudiced against gays and lesbians
but there is no point in trying to delude
myself that I feel anything but revulsion at
the idea of touching another man.

David Blunkett MP

The majority of these men are homosexual –
perhaps not the majority, but in the USA
there are already twenty-five per cent of
them and in England and Germany it is the
same. You cannot imagine it in the history
of France.

Edith Cresson, French Prime Minister

HOOLIGANISM

English football fans have become the
targets of everyone from ordinary police to

known Mafia enforcers from Argentina. Football matches are now the substitute for medieval tournaments and it's perfectly natural that some of the fans should be obstreperous.

Alan Clark MP

HOPE

I'm hopeful until the last hour of the last minute.

Alex Kitson, Deputy General Secretary of the Transport and General Workers' Union

HOUSING

There is no housing shortage in Lincoln today – just a rumour that is put about by people who have nowhere to live.

Councillor Murfin, Lord Mayor of Lincoln

Homelessness is homelessness no matter where you live.

Glenda Jackson MP

It is a scandal that there are two and a half homeless people in America.

Governor Michael Dukakis of Massachusetts

Home is important. It's important to have a home.

President George W. Bush

People are not homeless if they're sleeping in the streets of their own hometowns.

Vice President Dan Quayle

HUMAN BEINGS

I am a person who recognises the fallacy of humans.

President George W. Bush

HUMAN LIFE

Life is very important to Americans.

Senator Bob Dole of Kansas, US presidential candidate

Those who survived the San Francisco earthquake said, 'Thank God I'm still alive'. But, of course, those who died, their lives will never be the same again.

Representative Barbara Boxer of California

The loss of life will be irreplaceable.

Vice President Dan Quayle

It's important for us to explain to our nation that life is important. It's not only life of babies, but it's life of children living in, you know, the dark dungeons of the internet.

President George W. Bush

A single death is a tragedy, a million deaths is a statistic.

Joseph Stalin

HUMAN NATURE

You can tell a lot about a fellow's character by whether he picks out all of one colour or just grabs a handful.

President Ronald Reagan, explaining why he liked to have a jar of jellybeans on his desk

HUMILITY

I cannot tell you how grateful I am. I am filled with humidity.

Texas House of Representatives Speaker Gib Lewis

I have difficulty looking humble for extended periods of time.

Henry Kissinger, US Secretary of State

HUNGARY

You can't have been here long. You haven't got a pot-belly.

Prince Philip, speaking to an English tourist in Hungary

IDEOLOGY

What we're not going to do is set down an ideology on tablets of stone and wave it in the air.

Ian Wrigglesworth MP

I haven't read Karl Marx. I got stuck on that footnote on page two.

Harold Wilson, Prime Minister

IMAGINATION

Interviewer: Could you imagine yourself ever supporting a single currency?

Peter Lilley MP: I have such a fertile imagination I can imagine almost anything.

IMMIGRANTS

I had sixteen of them for lunch at the House of Commons.

Cyril Smith MP, discussing immigrants

We must be mad, literally mad, as a nation to be permitting the annual inflow of some 50,000 dependants of immigrants. As I look ahead I am filled with foreboding. Like the Roman, I see the River Tiber foaming with much blood.

Enoch Powell MP in 1968

Would you like foreigners to come into your house, settle down and help themselves to your fridge?

Jean-Louis Debre, French Interior Minister, on immigrants in 1997

I think God made all people good. But if we had to take a million immigrants in, say, Zulus next year, or Englishmen, and put them in Virginia, what group would be easier to assimilate and would cause less problems for the people of Virginia?

Pat Buchanan, presidential candidate, in 1991

INDUSTRY

At Consett you have got one of the best steelworks in Europe. It doesn't employ as many people as it used to because it is so modern.

Kenneth Clarke MP, speaking in 1995. The steelworks closed in 1980

The new Margam Colliery has yet to get off the ground.

Arthur Scargill, President of the National Union of Mineworkers

I think Consett is also one of the major centres for disposable baby nappies as well.

Kenneth Clarke MP, speaking in 1995. The nappy factory closed in 1991

INSULTS

Stanley Baldwin was an epileptic corpse.

Winston Churchill, Prime Minister

Malcolm Fraser looks like an Easter Island statue with an arse full of razor blades.

Paul Keating, Australian Prime Minister

You are a silly, rude bitch and since you are a potential breeder, God help the next generation.

Sir Nicholas Fairbairn MP, to a female heckler

Lady Astor told me that if I were her husband, she would put poison in my tea. I retorted by saying that if I were her husband, I would drink it.

Winston Churchill, Prime Minister

Dan Quayle is an empty suit that goes to funerals and plays golf.

Ross Perot, US presidential candidate

A pudgy puffball.

Alan Clark MP on Ken Clarke

Might as well have a corncob up his arse.

Alan Clark MP on Douglas Hurd

Bloody silly fool!

Prince Philip to a Cambridge University car park attendant who failed to recognise him

My opponent can compress the most words into the fewest ideas of anyone I've ever known.

President Abraham Lincoln

Charles de Gaulle looks like a female llama surprised in her bath.

Winston Churchill, Prime Minister

Gladstone has not got one redeeming defect.

Benjamin Disraeli, Prime Minister

I don't like Clarke and I don't trust
Heseltine. Clarke's a bounder and
Heseltine's a spiv.

**Sir Nicholas Fairbairn MP, on Kenneth Clarke
and Michael Heseltine**

I was thinking of you last night, Helmut,
because I was watching the sumo wrestling
on television.

**President Bill Clinton, greeting
Chancellor Kohl in 1994**

Margaret Thatcher adds the diplomacy of Alf
Garnett to the economics of Arthur Daley.

Denis Healey MP

In his usual arrogant and high-handed
fashion, he dons his Thatcherite jackboots
and stamps all over local opinion. He is like
Hitler with a beer belly.

Tony Banks MP on Kenneth Clarke MP

Ozone Man, Ozone. He's crazy, way out, far
out, man.

George Bush, Sr., speaking about Al Gore

A self-made man who worships his creator.

John Bright MP on Benjamin Disraeli MP

He and his colleagues are like hungry
hounds galloping after a red herring.

William Shelton MP

Robin Cook is the only Foreign Secretary in
seven hundred years who has more trouble
at home than he has abroad. But don't mock.
One day his looks will go.

John Major, former Prime Minister

Michael Foot is a kind of walking obituary
for the Labour Party.

Chris Patten MP

That man walks rather strangely. He has
either got a bad tailor, suffers from piles or
he's shit himself.

Lord Tebbit, on David Winnick MP

Unreconstructed wankers.

**Tony Blair, Prime Minister, on
the Scottish media**

INTEGRITY

Anyone in his position needs to be whiter than white.

Dame Jill Knight MP, on Nelson Mandela

INTERNATIONAL DEVELOPMENT

If you're at a summit, you're trying to climb a mountain.

Lord Carrington

What is the use of all these countries sending us aid, and then below the table kicking us in the teeth?

Anon. Thai economic spokesman

We must have adequate professional forces to impose our will on the Third World. Let me repeat that, because it is a very unfashionable thing to say. There are those moments in life when we are going to disagree with other people, and it is my belief that when we fundamentally disagree with someone we should win.

Newt Gingrich, Speaker of the House of Representatives

IRELAND

Ladies and gentlemen, if this coercion measure is passed, no man in Ireland will be able to speak upon politics unless he is born deaf and dumb.

Lord Charles Russell MP

If it weren't for these troubles, Ireland would be a very happy place.

Lord Brookeborough

Ireland has food and climate well matched for each other: dull. While Ireland is undoubtedly a great place to visit, living and working here is something else.

Robin Berrington, Cultural Affairs and Press Officer at the American Embassy in Dublin

Ireland is overrun by absentee landlords.

Sir Boyle Roche MP

So long as Ireland remains silent on this question, England will be deaf to our entreaties.

Anon. nineteenth-century Irish politician

At present, there are such goings on in Ireland that everything is at a standstill.

Sir Boyle Roche MP

After the next election, we have to give the third, and I hope last, deathblow to Home Rule.

Edward Stanley, Earl of Derby

I would like to see the two sisters embrace each other like one brother.

Sir Boyle Roche MP, on the relationship between England and Ireland

He would not rest satisfied until the rocky mountains of Ireland became cultivated valleys.

Sir Boyle Roche MP

JAPAN

Japan is an important ally of ours. Japan and the United States of the Western industrialised capacity, sixty per cent of the GNP, two countries. That's a statement in and of itself.

Vice President Dan Quayle

LANGUAGE

To listen to some people in politics, you'd think 'nice' was a four-letter word.

David Steel MP

No one has a finer command of the English language than the person who keeps his mouth shut.

Representative Sam Rayburn of Texas

LATIN AMERICA

Well, I learned a lot. I went down to [Latin America] to find out from them and learn their views. You'd be surprised. They're all individual countries.

President Ronald Reagan

The US has a vital interest in that area of the country.

Vice President Dan Quayle, on Latin America

I was recently on a tour of Latin America, and the only regret I have was that I didn't study Latin harder in school so I could converse with those people.

Vice President Dan Quayle

LAW AND ORDER

I can definitely say that had the police not been there this morning, there would have been no arrests.

Arthur Scargill, President of the National Union of Mineworkers

The streets are safe in Philadelphia. It's only the people who make them unsafe.

Mayor Frank Rizzo of Philadelphia

LEADERSHIP

It just seems to me it all boils down to leadership. Not that I'm such a great leader, but I think I'm at least an inch or two above the others. And that's going to be our message.

Newt Gingrich, Speaker of the House of Representatives

I have a different vision of leadership. A leadership is someone who brings people together.

President George W. Bush

The essence of being a Prime Minister is to have large ears.

Michael Heseltine MP

LEGISLATION

I will turn directly to the Asylum Bill later.

John Major, Prime Minister

This amendment does more damage than it does harm.

Representative Cynthia Willard-Lewis of New Orleans

Can't living with the Bill means it won't become law.

President George W. Bush

This Bill enables the Secretary of State to plunge into the waters of local government with his head firmly buried in the sand.

Baroness Burke

I can't think of any new law or existing law that's in force that wasn't before.

President George Bush, Sr.

Mr Speaker, this Bill is phoney with a
capital F.

Anon. US Congressman

LIES

A few months ago, I told the American
people I did not trade arms for hostages. My
heart and my best intentions still tell me
that's true, but the facts and the evidence tell
me it is not.

President Ronald Reagan

I was not lying. I said things that later on
seemed to be untrue.

President Richard Nixon

I am the nicest person I know and what I say
is the truth as I see it.

Peter Mandelson MP

Interviewer: You can't tell the truth all the
time, can you?

John Prescott MP: No, nobody does.

I was provided with additional input that was radically different from the truth. I assisted in furthering that version.

Colonel Oliver North, from his Iran-Contra testimony

In exceptional cases it is necessary to say something that is untrue to the House of Commons. The House of Commons understands that and has always accepted that.

William Waldegrave MP

Half the lies our opponents tell about us are not true.

Sir Boyle Roche MP

It contains a misleading impression, not a lie. It was being economical with the truth.

Sir Robert Armstrong, Cabinet Secretary and Head of the Civil Service

There are two kinds of truth. There are real truths, and there are made-up truths.

Mayor Marion Barry of Washington DC

I have lied in good faith.

Bernard Tapie, former French minister

Labour are pushing lies through our doorstep.

William Waldegrave MP

Four-fifths of the perjury in the world is expended on tomb-stones, women and competitors.

Lord Dewar

LOYALTY

I've always had a great respect and been very candid with her, and I hope the reverse is the case.

Chris Patten MP, on Margaret Thatcher

Interviewer: With John Redwood declaring, what do you do now? Do you stand back and say, 'Let the best man win'?

Jeremy Hanley MP: No, I don't. I'm right behind the Prime Minister.

I'm a cringing coward. I always vote the way they tell me to vote. I'm a balls-achingly, tooth-grindingly, butt-clenchingly loyal apparatchik.

Stephen Pound MP

The President doesn't want yes-men and yes-women around him. When he says no, we all say no.

Elizabeth Dole, US politician

I have had the most wonderfully loyal and supportive support from the Prime Minister.

Sir Michael Havers

MARRIAGE

A husband should tell his wife everything that he is sure she will find out, and before anyone else does.

Lord Dewar

I don't think a prostitute is more moral than a wife, but they are doing the same thing.

Prince Philip

MATHEMATICS

Interviewer: What's eight times seven?

Stephen Byers MP: I thought you would ask me that. I think it's fifty-four.

We've tripled the amount of money. I believe it's from $50 million up to $195 million available.

President George W. Bush

Other than when playing darts, I become confused at the mere mention of figures.

Neil Kinnock MP

MEDIA

It's been such a long journey, so many twenty-four hour days, and there are so many times I'd see you scrambling for a bus in the darkness or shivering in your parkas on a tarmac somewhere at dawn, and I'd think, 'That's tough. Too bad. It's not my problem. Get a job. Get a haircut.'

President George Bush, Sr., bidding farewell to reporters on his press plane

Not a single human being has asked me about the selection process – only journalists.

Frank Dobson MP

The BBC must blow their own trumpet and
have others blow their own trumpet for
them.

Paul Boateng MP

MEMORY

If you don't say anything, you won't be
called on to repeat it.

President Calvin Coolidge

I will never forget the '81 – or was it '82? –
honours list.

Julian Critchley MP

There are an awful lot of things I don't
remember.

President George Bush, Sr.

It is dangerous for a national candidate to
say things people might remember.

Senator Eugene McCarthy

MEN

One of the things that being in politics has taught me is that men are not a reasoned or reasonable sex.

Margaret Thatcher, Prime Minister

MIDDLE EAST

My administration has been calling upon all the leaders in the Middle East to do everything they can to stop the violence, to tell the different parties involved that peace will never happen.

President George W. Bush

The global importance of the Middle East is that it keeps the Near East and the Far East from encroaching on each other.

Vice President Dan Quayle

I wouldn't say she was open-minded on the Middle East so much as empty-headed. For instance, she probably thinks that Sinai is the plural of sinus.

Jonathan Aitken MP, on Margaret Thatcher

MISTAKES

It is perfectly American to be wrong.

Newt Gingrich, Speaker of the House of Representatives

The first mistake in politics is the going into it.

Benjamin Franklin, US statesman

There is a winter you know about in Russia. Hitler forgot about this. He must have been very loosely educated. We all hear about it at school, but he forgot it. I have never made such a bad mistake as that.

Winston Churchill, Prime Minister

I am being frank about myself in this book. I tell of my first mistake on page 850.

Henry Kissinger, US Secretary of State

Watergate was worse than a crime – it was a blunder.

Former President Richard Nixon

MIXED METAPHORS

Well, you can only fire at an open goal when you discover that it is a hand grenade you are kicking rather than the ball.

David Blunkett MP

If we haven't got razor-edged salesmen on the coalface nowadays, nobody's going to buy the bacon.

Albert Reynolds, Irish Prime Minister

That's Washington. That's the place where you find people getting ready to jump out of the foxholes before the first shot is fired.

President George W. Bush

We have slammed shut the revolving door we found open.

Irish Prime Minister Bertie Ahern

It's an idea someone picks up and runs with only to find they've painted themselves into a corner.

Anon. Labour Party spokesman

That particular honeymoon has completely burst.

Virginia Bottomley MP

I know I'm treading into a minefield and I'll have to sink or swim.

Anne Smith

The Americans have sowed the seed, and now they have reaped the whirlwind.

Sebastian Coe, before he became an MP

That wasn't the only thing he did. That was just the froth on the cake.

Julian Critchley MP

The Government are shrugging their feet over this issue.

Doug Hoyle MP

It is a hothouse in a goldfish bowl.

Neil Kinnock MP

It's not something you can do like a fairy godmother from the top of a Christmas tree.

Michael Heseltine MP

The Government will not be held to ransom by a lot of flotsam and bobtail.

Norman Lamont MP

Paddy Ashdown was dealt a difficult pack of cards – but he kept his eye on the ball all the way through.

Charles Kennedy MP

No one wants to say the sky is falling, but in this instance I am afraid the emperor has no clothes. Despite Herculean efforts by the Council and Council staff, we are still only dealing with the tip of the iceberg.

Charles Millard, NYC Councilman

When shall the lion of autocracy walk hand in hand with the floodgates of democracy?

James Sexton MP

It's almost like a guillotine – the trap door opens and you're gone.

Ken Livingstone MP

That's a fascinating crystal ball, but I'll tell you the other side of the coin.

Lord Archer

One doesn't know how many hot potatoes will appear over the horizon.

Sir David Madel MP

The Militants in Liverpool spend money like water, as if it came from outer space.

Rhodes Boyson MP

Deputy Sweetman had better give up pretending to be a cuckoo sitting on a mare's nest.

Sean MacEntee, Irish politician

The Home Secretary has nailed his flag to the wall.

Don Concannon MP

The Secretary of State has taken the brakes off the logjam.

Christine Hancock, General Secretary of the Royal College of Nursing

I can smell a rat. I can see him floating in the air, but mark me – I shall nip him in the bud.

Sir Boyle Roche MP

Since the government has let the cat out of the bag there is nothing else to do but take the bull by the horns.

Jeremiah MacVeagh MP

Everyone in the town hall is wandering around like headless chickens looking over their shoulders to see if they are going to be next.

Anon. Hackney local government officer

Our members will be grasping the bull by the horns only to find that it's a damp squib.

Anon. Trade Union leader

If you open that Pandora's box, you never know what Trojan horses will jump out.

Ernest Bevin MP

It is no use for the honourable Member to shake his head in the teeth of his own words.

William E. Gladstone, Prime Minister

Clearly the Prime Minister's devious hand is afoot.

John Smith MP

MONEY

It's your money. You paid for it.

President George W. Bush

Yes, it's the politics of envy. We're envious of company directors' wealth. These people are stinking lousy thieving incompetent scum.

Frank Dobson MP

MORALITY

Christian monogamy and its assumption of fidelity is as fallacious as the Catholic concept of the chastity of priests. I am sure that polygamy and harems probably worked better. We live in a priggish and prim age.

Sir Nicholas Fairbairn MP

MUSIC

How could I? I know only two tunes. One of them is Yankee Doodle and the other isn't.

President Ulysses Grant, upon being asked if he had enjoyed the music at a concert

What do you gargle with? Pebbles?

Prince Philip, speaking to singer Tom Jones

The guy over there at Pease – a woman actually – she said something about a country-western song about the train, a light at the end of the tunnel. I only hope it's not a train coming the other way. Well, I said to her, well, I'm a country music fan. I love it, always have. Doesn't fit the mould of some of the columnists, I might add, but nevertheless – of what they think I ought to fit in, but I love it. You should have been there with me at the CMA awards at Nashville. But nevertheless, I said to them there's another one that the Nitty Ditty Nitty Gritty Great Bird – and it says if you want to see a rainbow you've got to stand a little rain. We've had a little rain. New Hampshire has had too much rain.

President George Bush, Sr.

NAMES

I am profoundly grateful to Prime Minister Brown ... Blair.

President Bill Clinton

We've never had a President named Bob. I think it's about time we had one.

**Senator Bob Dole of Kansas,
US presidential candidate**

She's just trying to make sure Anthony gets a good meal – Antonio.

**President George W. Bush, on his wife
inviting Justice Antonin Scalia to dinner at
the White House**

Ladies and gentlemen, the President of the United States – Hoobert Heever.

**Harry von Zell, US radio announcer,
attempting to introduce President Herbert
Hoover**

The great President who might have been – Hubert Horatio Hornblower.

**President Jimmy Carter, attempting to
introduce Hubert H. Humphrey**

I'd like to extend a warm welcome to Chairman Moe.

**President Ronald Reagan, welcoming
President Doe of Liberia**

But I mustn't go on singling out names. One must not be a name-dropper, as Her Majesty remarked to me yesterday.

Norman St. John Stevas MP

NEGOTIATION

It is at times a minefield.

Stan Orme MP, on negotiations between the National Union of Mineworkers and the National Coal Board during the miners' strike

We haven't demanded anything. What we have demanded is that the coal board withdraw their demands.

Arthur Scargill, President of the National Union of Mineworkers

NEUTRALITY

Neutrality doesn't make sense – who are they neutral against?

Denis Healey MP

I will sit on the fence if it is strong enough.

Cyril Smith MP

NICARAGUA

The most covert activity known to man is what the United States is doing in Nicaragua.

Admiral Stansfield Turner

NORTHERN IRELAND

Anyone who isn't confused in Northern Ireland doesn't really understand the problem.

John Hume MP

I'm sick of answering questions about the fucking peace process.

John Bruton, Irish Prime Minister

Decommissioning is the perpetual rock upon which we have come adrift.

Peter Mandelson MP

The people of Northern Ireland should take a step back and ask themselves whether they have moved forwards.

Tony Blair, Prime Minister

The absolute rejection of it automatically, a sort of Pavlova's dog reaction, was regrettable.

David Penhaligon MP, on the 1985 Anglo-Irish peace initiative

NUCLEAR POWER

Our nuclear power stations are as safe as they can possibly be, and are getting safer all the time.

Sir Hugh Rossi MP

A nuclear power plant is definitely safer than eating, because three hundred people choke to death on food every year.

Governor Dixie Lee Ray of Washington State

It's too bad it didn't happen closer to the Kremlin.

Senator Steven Symms of Idaho, on the Chernobyl accident

OIL

If the price of conventional oil is X, you have a price of X plus Y for the non-conventional oil, and the international price – you know what that is – but we have indicated we will continue to subsidise the prices. So that what you would end up with would be a mix of these prices.

Marc Lalonde, Canadian energy minister, explaining his government's energy policy

The price of oil is not determined by the British Parliament. It is determined by some lads riding camels who do not even know how to spell 'national sovereignty'.

Lord Feather

Interviewer: Does it all boil down to a barrel of oil at the end of the day?

David Mellor MP: Well, I think that's a crude way of putting it.

OPINIONS

My general approach is that you mustn't generalise.

Harriet Harman MP

I have my own opinions, strong opinions,
but I don't always agree with them.

President George Bush, Sr.

OPPORTUNITY

This is a window of opportunity for us to
step into.

Tom King MP

OPTIMISM

I see this glass not half-empty, but half-full,
and more.

President George Bush, Sr.

My project will be complete when the
Labour Party learns to love Peter Mandelson.

Tony Blair, Prime Minister

There are no American infidels in Baghdad.
Never!

**Mohammed Saeed al-Sahaf, Iraqi
Minister of Information**

ORATORY

Our Party. New Labour. Our Mission. New Britain. New Britain. New Labour. New Britain. New Britain.

Tony Blair, Prime Minister

And so, in my State of the – my State of the Union – or state – my speech to the nation, whatever you want to call it, speech to the nation – I asked Americans to give 4,000 years – 4,000 hours over the next – the rest of your life – of service to America. That's what I asked – 4,000 hours.

President George W. Bush

That speech must have affected every thinking Conservative MP and many others as well.

David Howell MP

This is no time for soundbites, but I feel the hand of history on my shoulder.

Tony Blair, Prime Minister

A soundbite never buttered a parsnip.

John Major, former Prime Minister

You people are exemplifying what my brother meant when he said in his inaugural address, 'Ask what you can do for – er – do not ask what you can do – ask not what you can do for your country.' Well, anyhow, you remember his words. That's why my brother is President.

Robert Kennedy, US Attorney General

Winston Churchill devoted the best years of his life to preparing his impromptu speeches.

F. E. Smith MP

Well, my speech seems to have been a hit according to all the newspapers. It shows you never can tell. I thought it was rotten.

President Harry Truman

I am not one who – who flamboyantly believes in throwing a lot of words around.

President George Bush, Sr.

Verbosity leads to unclear, inarticulate things.

Vice President Dan Quayle

Somebody – somebody asked me, what's it take to win? I said to them, I can't remember, what does it take to win the Super Bowl? Or maybe Steinbrenner, my friend George, will tell us what it takes for the Yanks to win – one run! But I went over to the Strawberry Festival this morning, and ate a piece of shortcake over there, able to enjoy it right away, and once I completed it, it didn't have to be approved by Congress – I just went ahead and ate it. And that leads me into what I want to talk to you about today.

President George Bush, Sr.

The honourable member's speech reminds me of Columbus. When he set out, he didn't know where he was going. When he got there, he didn't know where he was. And when he returned home, he didn't know where he'd been.

Winston Churchill, Prime Minister

PAGERS

I can have no objections to instruments that merely vibrate.

Speaker Betty Boothroyd, speaking to the House of Commons about pagers

PARANOIA

I have information that the Government is planning to have me certified by psychiatrists.

Reverend Ian Paisley MP

PARENTHOOD

Bringing up children on your own is very difficult, even where there are two parents.

Virginia Bottomley MP

Republicans understand the importance of bondage between parent and child.

Vice President Dan Quayle

PARLIAMENT

The House of Commons is the longest running farce in the West End.

Cyril Smith MP

Anybody who enjoys being in the House of Commons probably needs psychiatric help.

Ken Livingstone MP

The House of Lords is a model of how to care for the elderly.

Frank Field MP

The cure for admiring the House of Lords is to go and look at it.

Walter Bagehot

PARTY CONFERENCES

Party Conferences are the chance for the grass roots to get their hobbyhorses off their chest.

Anon. Liberal Democrat spokesman

PATIENCE

I am extraordinarily patient, provided I get my own way in the end.

Margaret Thatcher, Prime Minister

PAST

I have always said it is a great mistake ever to pre-judge the past.

William Whitelaw MP

The only way to prevent what's past is to put a stop to it before it happens.

Sir Boyle Roche MP

Oh look – with hindsight, you can always look back.

Lord Young

That part of it is behind us now. I'm drawing a line under the sand.

John Major, Prime Minister

I think we agree, the past is over.

President George W. Bush

PEERAGES

It's like a vasectomy – you can have all the fun without any of the responsibility.

Stephen Norris MP commenting on the benefits of a peerage

PENSIONERS

Buy long johns, check your hot-water bottles, knit gloves and scarves and get your grandchildren to give you a woolly night-cap.

Edwina Currie MP, giving advice to pensioners on how to deal with winter cold

Interviewer: Why can't you answer my question on old age pensions?

Michael Heseltine MP: I'm not entitled to an old age pension.

PERSEVERANCE

When your back is against the wall, the only thing to do is turn around and fight.

John Major, Prime Minister

This is Preservation Month. I appreciate preservation. It's what you do when you run for President. You've got to preserve.

President George W. Bush, speaking during Perseverance Month

This is still the greatest country in the world, if we just steel our wills and lose our minds.

President Bill Clinton

PERSONAL EXPERIENCE

If experience is the name that people give to their mistakes, then I have that experience.

John Major, Prime Minister

In the case of my own case, this has not been the case.

Peter Tatchell, gay rights campaigner

Those who lived through the Falklands crisis – and I am one of them ...

Francis Pym MP

Everyone in politics ought to be arrested at least once. It's an education.

Alan Clark MP

PERSONALITY

Let me put it to you this way, I am not a revengeful person.

President George W. Bush

POLAND

My fellow Americans, yesterday the Polish government, a military dictatorship, a bunch of no-good lousy bums ...

President Ronald Reagan, in a voice test for a radio statement that was inadvertently broadcast

In Poland, or some other South American country ...

Arthur Scargill, President of the National Union of Mineworkers

POLICE

It is asking too much to require the police to stand there like sitting ducks while wild men throw petrol bombs at them.

Eldon Griffiths MP

Get this thing straight once and for all. The policeman isn't there to create disorder. The policeman is there to preserve disorder.

Mayor Richard J. Daley of Chicago

The police force in Britain is a reactionary force. It has to respond.

Michael Shersby MP

There's nothing wrong with this country that we couldn't cure by turning it over to the police for a couple of weeks.

Governor George Wallace of Alabama

POLITICIANS

Many MPs never see the London that exists beyond the wine bars and brothels of Westminster.

Ken Livingstone MP

Politics would be a helluva good business if it weren't for the goddamned people.

President Richard Nixon

Ninety per cent of politicians give the other ten per cent a bad reputation.

Henry Kissinger, US Secretary of State

POLITICS

Politics is show business for ugly people.

Paul Begala, White House senior adviser, campaign adviser to Bill Clinton

Politics is a bit like bicycling. If you keep bicycling, you'll get there in the end.

John Major, Prime Minister

It's like a game of chess: all the cards are thrown in the air, the board's turned over and you're in a whole new ball game.

Anthony Howard, political commentator

We have got to all work together in the national interest and get away from the everyday bump and grind of politics.

Paddy Ashdown MP, who admitted to an affair with his secretary

I used to say that politics is the second oldest profession, and I have come to know that it bears a gross similarity to the first.

President Ronald Reagan

To break the two party monopoly will be very difficult.

David Owen MP

POVERTY

The chief problem of the low income farmers is poverty.

Governor Nelson Rockefeller of New York

We're the only nation in the world where all our poor people are fat.

Senator Phil Gramm of Texas

The poor man was absolutely robbed by that accursed Tithe Bill, by fully one-tenth of his hard earnings. Nay, he was sometimes deprived of as much as one-twentieth.

Major O'Gorman MP

Money isn't everything, but it does make poverty tolerable.

Moss Evans, General Secretary of the General Workers' Union

When you've seen one ghetto area, you've seen them all.

Spiro Agnew, campaigning as Nixon's running mate, 1968

POWER

I think we're making progress. We understand where the power of this country lay. It lays in the hearts and souls of Americans. It must lay in our pocketbooks. It lays in the willingness for people to work hard. But as importantly, it lays in the fact that we've got citizens from all walks of life, all political parties, that are willing to say, I want to love my neighbour. I want to make somebody's life just a little bit better.

President George W. Bush

Interviewer: What do you mean when you say that Mikhail Gorbachev appears to assert complete control over the Soviet government?

George Bush, Sr.: I was with him, and I sensed – er – stop! And we stopped. And he got out of the car. So, he controls the agenda. And I saw that, yeah.

Power corrupts. Absolute power is kind of neat.

US Secretary of the Navy John Lehman

PRAISE

He is a committed pederast.

Tom Levitt MP, attempting to describe a teacher as 'a committed pedagogue'

Laura and I are proud to call John and Michelle Engler our friends. I know you're proud to call him governor. What a good man the Englers are.

President George W. Bush

A great man? Why, he's selfish, he's arrogant, he thinks he's the centre of the universe – yes, you're right. He is a great man.

Winston Churchill, Prime Minister, on Charles de Gaulle

Every Prime Minister should have a Willie.

**Margaret Thatcher, Prime Minister,
attempting to praise William Whitelaw MP**

I like old Joe Stalin. He's straightforward.

President Harry Truman

I believe Stalin is truly representative of the
heart and soul of Russia, and I believe that
we are going to get along very well with him
and the Russian people.

President Franklin Roosevelt

I would have to ask the questioner. I haven't
had a chance to ask the questioners the
question they've been questioning. On the
other hand, I firmly believe she'll be a fine
secretary of labour. And I've got confidence
in Linda Chavez. She is a – she'll bring an
interesting perspective to the Labour
Department.

President George W. Bush

Mr Macmillan is the best Prime Minister we
have.

R. A. Butler MP

He has certainly earned a reputation as a
fantastic mayor, because the results speak for
themselves. I mean, New York's a safer place
for him to be.

President George W. Bush

I do remain confident in Linda. She'll make a
fine labour secretary. From what I've read in
the press accounts, she's perfectly qualified.

**President George W. Bush, commenting on
Linda Chavez**

So great a man, and so wise a ruler.

Winston Churchill, on Mussolini, in 1935

PREDICTIONS

It's difficult to make predictions, particularly
about the future.

**Anon. Representative of the UN High
Commission for Refugees**

We can beat the Liberals even with one
engine tied behind our backs.

**Joe Clark, Conservative Prime Minister
of Canada**

It'll permanently damage relations for a long time.

Jimmy Knapp, leader of the Railwaymen's Union

I'm gonna be so tough as mayor I'm gonna make Attila the Hun look like a faggot.

Mayor Frank Rizzo of New York

This is the first step in a chain that will unfold.

David Mellor MP

I've found the future rather difficult to predict before it happens.

Lord Jenkins

I would expect things to go on much as they are, until there is some change.

Sir Anthony Parsons, foreign policy adviser to Margaret Thatcher

If there is a leadership challenge, it will take place.

Kenneth Baker MP

The first black President will be a politician who is black.

Governor L. Douglas Wilder of Virginia

The future will be better tomorrow.

Vice President Al Gore

Single misfortunes never come alone, and the greatest of all national calamities is generally followed by one greater.

Sir Boyle Roche MP

I don't make predictions. I never have and I never will.

Tony Blair, Prime Minister

PREPARATION

The right honourable gentleman has done what I would like you all to do – when you lay an egg, save it for a rainy day.

Robert Thwaites MP

I think that ministers over the years have not seen this problem coming, because it has been coming for a long time.

Nicholas Soames MP

One word sums up the responsibility of any Vice President. And that word is 'to be prepared'.

Vice President Dan Quayle

We are not ready for any unforeseen event that may or may not occur.

Vice President Dan Quayle

PRESIDENCY

The most important part of the job is not to be governor, or first lady in my case.

President George W. Bush

I think the American public wants a solemn ass as President and I think I'll go along with them.

President Calvin Coolidge

Now that Bobby has been assassinated,
Teddy must run for the Presidency.

Rose Kennedy

What's wrong with being a boring kind of
guy? I think to kind of suddenly try to get
my hair coloured, dance up and down in a
mini-skirt or do something to show that I've
got a lot of jazz out there and drop a bunch
of one-liners – we're talking about the
President of the United States. I kind of think
I'm a scintillating kind of fellow.

President George Bush, Sr.

If the Soviet empire still existed, I'd be
terrified. The fact is, we can afford a fairly
ignorant presidency now.

**Newt Gingrich, Speaker of the
House of Representatives**

Interviewer: Why would you make a good
President?

George Bush, Sr.: Well, I've got a big family,
and lots of friends.

I may not have been the greatest President,
but I've had the most fun eight years.

President Bill Clinton

Interviewer: Mr Vice President, if you were to suddenly become President, do you think you would be up to the job?

Dan Quayle: If such an unfortunate thing were to happen, yes, I believe I would be.

PRINCIPLES

I know what I believe. I will continue to articulate what I believe and what I believe. I believe what I believe is right.

President George W. Bush

By the way, you ought to know that my public pronouncements bear no relation to my private views and there are three things I cannot stand – God, the Queen and family.

Sir John Foster MP

When you say that you agree to a thing in principle, you mean that you have not the slightest intention of carrying it out in practice.

Otto von Bismarck

As a senator, you always had a lot of wiggle room. You could say one thing in the morning and take it back in the afternoon. That was sort of standard operating procedure. Here you don't make a statement and then decide to take it back. Words live with you.

Vice President Dan Quayle

One reason I changed the Labour Party is so that we can remain true to our principles.

Tony Blair, Prime Minister

I don't have to accept their tenants. I was trying to convince them to accept my tenants.

President George W. Bush

My friends, no matter how rough the road may be, we can and we will never, never surrender to what is right.

Vice President Dan Quayle

If I invade Mars, the Labour Party will invade Mars. From their point of view, Mars today, Cadbury tomorrow and Bourneville the day after. Heaven above knows where they will go next.

John Major, Prime Minister

Anybody in my job steers a tightrope
between being popular and being principled.

Virginia Bottomley MP

PRIORITIES

The more important things are more
important than the less important.

Stephen Dorrell MP

PRISONS

Prison is and never has been a soft option.

Ann Widdecombe MP

Mr Lewis has been head of the Prison Service
for two years and during that time a great
deal of progress has been made, particularly
in terms of escapes.

Michael Howard MP

We have no political prisoners, only
communists and others involved in
conspiracies against the country.

South Korean President Park Chung-Lee

How nice to see you all here.

**Roy Jenkins MP, speaking to prisoners whilst
visiting a prison in London**

There's a lot of overcrowded prisons in the
south, and we're planning a new one.

Douglas Hurd MP

It's my personal belief that if they're not
rehabilitated after fifteen years, kill 'em.

**Senator Tim Jennings of New Mexico,
on prisoners**

If the criminal wants to commit suicide, then
he should be allowed to do so. Something
should be left in the cell. Perhaps a razor
blade.

**Jonathan Guinness, Conservative candidate in
the Lincoln by-election, 1973**

We do not have any political prisoners. We
have political internal exiles.

Chilean President Augusto Pinochet, in 1975

PRIVATISATION

Nicholas Ridley is going to sell off the
nation's water assets lock, stock and barrel.

Jack Cunningham MP

We've just had the biggest saturation
advertising on record to publicise the sale of
water.

Tony Blair MP

PROBLEMS

I am not part of the problem. I am a
Republican.

Vice President Dan Quayle

Now the only thing that remains unresolved
is the resolution of the problem.

Tom Wells, Ontario Education Minister

PROCREATION

It's one of the great urban myths that people
get pregnant in order to have children.

Menzies Campbell MP

You can't manufacture children overnight.

Jack Straw MP

Illegitimacy is something we should talk about in terms of not having it.

Vice President Dan Quayle

I note the tremendous progress of this city. The Mayor was telling me in the last twelve years, you have had practically a doubling of population. Where has this progress come from? That progress has not come primarily from government, but it has come from the activities of hundreds of thousands of individual Mississippians.

President Richard Nixon

PROGRESS

I believe we are on an irreversible trend towards more freedom and democracy. But that could change.

Vice President Dan Quayle

Britain was very different in my grandfather's day. There were children walking around without proper feet.

Lord Attlee

Sixty years of progress, without change.

Saudi Arabian Government slogan

We don't want to go back to tomorrow. We want to go forward.

Vice President Dan Quayle

PROMISES

Well, I think if you say you're going to do something and don't do it, that's trustworthiness.

President George W. Bush

Look, we are not making empty promises. This is a blueprint to create heaven on earth.

Peter Warburton, Deputy Leader of the National Law Party

This strategy represents our policy for all time. Until it's changed.

Marlin Fitzwater, White House press spokesman

Sometimes you can have competing election promises.

Malcolm Fraser, Australian Prime Minister

The President has kept all of the promises he intended to keep.

George Stephanopolous, aide to President Bill Clinton

PROTEST

Let this be a silent protest that will be heard throughout this country.

Mayor Tim Leddin of Limerick

PROVERBS

Cometh the hour, cometh the moment.

Charles Kennedy MP

You cannot roast a wet blanket.

Mackenzie King, Canadian Prime Minister

A leopard can never change his stripes.

Vice President Al Gore

It separates the sheep from the men.

Lord Puttnam

If Lincoln was alive today, he'd roll over in his grave.

President Gerald Ford

You know what they say – don't get mad, get angry.

Edwina Currie MP

If you give a man a fish he will fish for a day.

Vice President Dan Quayle

No one would go to Hitler's funeral if he were alive today.

Ron Brown MP

The foot is on the other feet.

Bertie Ahern, Irish Prime Minister

You can lead a dead horse to water, but you can't make him drink.

Mayor Allan Lamport of Toronto

Next week is another day.

Peadar Clohessy, Irish politician

PUBLIC OPINION

I have a thermometer in my mouth and I am listening to it all the time.

William Whitelaw MP

They said, 'You know, this issue doesn't seem to resignate with the people'. And I said, you know something? Whether it resignates or not doesn't matter to me, because I stand for doing what's the right thing, and what the right thing is hearing the voices of the people who work.

President George W. Bush

Jim Callaghan had a good ear for the wind blowing from the grass roots.

Shirley Williams MP

Many people feel that the Labour Party has gone out on a limb and lost its roots.

Rosie Barnes MP

PUBLICITY

Never forget your photographer when visiting a hospital – there may always be a patient who can manage a smile.

Virginia Bottomley MP

If I want to knock a story off the front page, I just change my hairstyle.

First Lady Hillary Clinton

That is a higher proportion than the percentage of the general public with whom I am familiar.

Peter Lilley MP, responding to a survey claiming that only two per cent of the public knew who he was

RACISM

I'm not against blacks, and a lot of the good blacks will attest to that.

Governor Evan Meechan of Arizona in 1990

The only reason we need ZIP codes is because niggers can't read.

Senator William Scott of Virginia in 1978

Some black bastard.

**David Evans, Conservative candidate
describing a local man accused of rape in 1997**

I am strongly of the opinion that Negroes
ought to be in Africa, yellow men in Asia,
and white men in Europe and America.

Harry Truman in 1911

Unfortunately, the people of Louisiana are
not racists.

Vice President Dan Quayle

It looks like it was put in by an Indian.

**Prince Philip commenting on a fuse box
whilst visiting a Scottish factory**

America must be kept American. Biological
laws show that Nordics deteriorate when
mixed with other races.

President Calvin Coolidge in 1921

I draw a line in the dust and toss the
gauntlet before the feet of tyranny. And I say
– segregation now, segregation tomorrow,
segregation forever.

Governor George Wallace of Alabama in 1963

You managed not to get eaten, then?

**Prince Philip to a student who had been
trekking in Papua New Guinea**

RAPE

I say this a lot, and I probably shouldn't: the
difference between rape and seduction is
salesmanship.

**Bill Carpenter, Mayor of Independence,
Missouri**

REALITY

I'm gonna talk about the ideal world. I've read
– I understand reality. If you're asking me as
the President, would I understand reality, I do.

President George W. Bush

REBELLION

Bringing the leadership to its knees
occasionally is a good way of keeping it on
its toes.

Tony Banks MP

RECESSION

A government is not an old pair of socks that you throw out. Come to think of it, you don't throw out old pairs of socks anyway these days.

Russian President Boris Yeltsin

The year ended with the concern for Americans that are hurting because of this sluggish economy. I mean, when families are having trouble making ends meet or are thinking even if they have a job, I might not have one tomorrow. Fear. You worry about that. I worry a lot about that.

President George Bush, Sr., in 1992

I don't want to run the risk of ruining what is a lovely recession.

President George Bush, Sr., attempting to say 'reception'

This state has gone through hell. It's gone through an extraordinarily difficult time, coming off a pinnacle, you might say, of low unemployment. Now, you're at about the national level. And yes, people are hurting. And I'm determined to turn it around. I told some of them over there – there's a big difference, you know. People say to me –

difference between domestic and foreign policy. How could you lead the world – and they gave me some credit for that in Desert Storm, that the American people still feel very, very strongly about – and – how can you do that and then have such difficulties with this economy?

President George Bush, Sr., to the people of New Hampshire

I've talked to you on a number of occasions about the economic problems our nation faces, and I'm prepared to tell you it's in a hell of a mess. We're not connected to the press room yet, are we?

President Ronald Reagan

We raised taxes on the American people and we put this country right into a recession.

Vice President Dan Quayle

The argument about Labour destroying any prospects of recovery may be déjà vu here, but it's certainly not déjà vu in the country. It's very much vu. It's very much what – er – it's very much – er – that shows what sort of education I had.

Chris Patten MP

We'll be heading for the deepening heights
of recession.

Anon. Liberal Democrat economic spokesman

I am less interested what the definition is.
You might argue technically, are we in a
recession or not. But when there's this kind
of sluggishness and concern – definitions,
heck with it.

President George Bush, Sr.

This President is going to lead us out of this
recovery.

Vice President Dan Quayle

RELIGION

You cannot be the President of the United
States if you don't have faith. Remember
Lincoln, going to his knees in times of trial
and the Civil War and all that stuff. You
can't be. And we are blessed. So don't feel
sorry for me – don't cry for me, Argentina.
Message – I care.

President George Bush, Sr.

Black preachers start out not intending to make sense. They create a kind of psychological connection. You end up crying. You end up feeling good. You end up thinking about your mom, and you go away fulfilled. But you're not better off.

Mayor Andrew Young of Atlanta

Saint Patrick was a Protestant.

Reverend Ian Paisley MP

Our priorities is our faith.

President George W. Bush

God ordained that I should be the next President of the United States.

President Woodrow Wilson

Islam is not a pacifist religion. Islam will hit back, and sometimes hit back first.

Kalim Saddiqui, spokesman for a militant Islamic organisation

And so I understand New Hampshire because I have this wonderfully warm feeling that New Hampshire feels exactly the way we do on these questions of family values and faith. Somebody said to me, we prayed for you over there. That was not just because I threw up on the Prime Minister of Japan, either. Where was he when I needed him? I said, let me tell you something. And I say this – I don't know whether any ministers from the Episcopal Church are here – I hope so. But I said this to him – you're on to something here. It's been great. I'll go back to Washington all fired up for tomorrow and tackle the President or the Prime Minister of this or the Governor of that coming in. But I'll have this heartbeat.

President George Bush, Sr.

When an Englishman wants to get married, to whom does he go? To the clergy. When he wants to get his child baptised, to whom does he go? To the clergy. When he wants to get buried, to whom does he go?

William E. Gladstone, Prime Minister

RESPECT

I deserve respect for the things I did not do.

Vice President Dan Quayle

REPORTS

This white paper is a waste of the money it's printed on.

Matthew Taylor MP

RESIGNATION

That son of a bitch MacArthur isn't going to resign on me. I want him fired.

President Harry Truman

This isn't a man who is leaving with his head between his legs.

Vice President Dan Quayle, on the resignation of John Sununu

Jim Prior's his own man. We all are.

Sir Humphrey Atkins, commenting on Jim Prior's decision to resign

RESPONSIBILITY

I don't blame anyone, except perhaps all of us.

William Whitelaw MP

It's no use trying to pin a donkey on a few individuals, however much Lord Justice Scott wants to.

Alan Clark MP

I want each and every American to know for certain that I'm responsible for the decisions I make, and each of you are as well.

President George W. Bush

RIGHTS

We expect [the Salvadorans] to work towards the elimination of human rights in accordance with the pursuit of justice.

Vice President Dan Quayle

The right to suffer is one of the joys of a free economy.

Howard Pyle, aide to President Dwight D. Eisenhower, commenting on unemployment in Detroit

The Civil Rights Act is the single most
dangerous piece of legislation ever
introduced in the Congress.

Senator Jesse Helms

It is about a socialist, anti-family political
movement that encourages women to leave
their husbands, kill their children, practice
witchcraft, destroy capitalism and become
lesbians.

**Pat Robertson, presidential candidate, on the
proposed Equal Rights Amendment in 1992**

I favour the Civil Rights Act of 1964 and it
must be enforced at gunpoint if necessary.

President Ronald Reagan

RIOTS

Who is to blame for the riots? The rioters!

Vice President Dan Quayle

RIVALRY

Well, on the manhood thing, I'll put mine up against his anytime.

President George Bush, Sr., replying to Walter Mondale's charge that he didn't 'have the manhood to apologise'

ROYALTY

Wasn't it too bad you sent your royal family to the guillotine?

Prince Philip, to the French Minister of the Interior

She is a lady short on looks, absolutely deprived of any dress sense, has a figure like a Jurassic monster, is very greedy when it comes to loot, has no tact, and wants to upstage everyone else.

Sir Nicholas Fairbairn MP, on the Duchess of York

If it doesn't fart or eat hay, she's not interested.

Prince Philip on Princess Anne

Britain has become godless. Man is made with a hollow which only God can fill. Then along came this false goddess and filled the gap for a time. But, like all false gods, she could not last. The British people identified with someone who had pretty loose morals and certainly loose sexual morals. A period of disillusionment is bound to set in.

Lord Coggan, on the death of Princess Diana

I feel she will be remembered for her role during wartime. She stood alone against the mighty Nazi army.

David Winnick MP on the Queen Mother

RUMOURS

I think I can scotch that one on the head straight away.

Sir Jeremy Thomas

RUSSIA

The Soviet Union would remain a one-party nation even if an opposition party were permitted – because everyone would join that party.

President Ronald Reagan

They're running away from communism toward our way of life because of television and basketball. You play basketball in this country for a month, you go back, you're never going to be happy waiting on line for a potato.

Governor Mario Cuomo of New York

The bastards murdered half my family.

Prince Philip on the Russians

SACKINGS

I did not desire to fire Mr Fitzgerald. I prefer to use the correct term, which is to abolish his job.

Robert Seamons, US Secretary for the Air Force

I did not drop him from the Cabinet. There was simply a new Government of which Mr Molloy was not a member.

Charles Haughey, Irish Prime Minister

SCOTLAND

How do you keep the natives off the booze
long enough to pass the test?

**Prince Philip, speaking to a Scottish
driving instructor**

SECRECY

We're not the sort of party that does deals
behind smoke-filled doors.

Bryan Gould MP

SELF-BELIEF

The longer I am out of office, the more
infallible I appear to myself.

Henry Kissinger, US Secretary of State

I would have made a good Pope.

President Richard Nixon

Do I have a mounting confidence that I could lead? You bet. Would I be a good President? I'd be crackerjack!

George Bush, Sr., campaigning for the presidency

SEX

Politics gives guys so much power that they tend to behave badly around women. And I hope I never get into that.

President Bill Clinton

The only safe pleasure for a Member of Parliament nowadays is a bag of boiled sweets.

Julian Critchley MP

I've had more women by accident than JFK had on purpose.

President Lyndon B. Johnson

She's a wonderful, wonderful person, and we're looking to a happy and wonderful night – er, life.

Senator Ted Kennedy, talking about his fiancée, Victoria Reggie

They don't call me Tyrannosaurus Sex for nothing.

Senator Ted Kennedy

I wonder how it is with you, Harold? If I don't have a woman for three days, I get a terrible headache.

President John F. Kennedy, to Prime Minister Harold Macmillan

I don't give a damn about protocol. I'm a swinger. Bring out the beautiful spies.

Henry Kissinger, US Secretary of State

I've looked on many women with lust. I've committed adultery in my heart many times. God knows I will do this and forgives me.

President Jimmy Carter, in an interview with Playboy

SHOCK

I was stunned with outrage.

Neil Kinnock MP

SILENCE

Mrs Thatcher's silence has resounded like thunder across Britain.

Paddy Ashdown MP

SLEAZE

There's no smoke without mud being flung around.

Edwina Currie MP

What we have is a person who was publicly discredited in public.

Paddy Ashdown MP

SLEEP

I never drink coffee at lunch. I find it keeps me awake for the afternoon.

President Ronald Reagan

SOCIAL POLICY

The government should provide fundamentals, like underwear, for the people at the bottom of society.

Roy Hattersley MP

There is a mandate to impose a voluntary return to traditional values.

President Ronald Reagan

The Labour Party want to destroy the bottom rung of the escalator.

Michael Howard MP

SOCIAL SECURITY

They want the federal government controlling Social Security like it's some kind of federal programme.

President George W. Bush

Social security scroungers should be made to give a pint of blood every six months.

Michael Brotherton MP

We want to dehumanise the social welfare system.

Albert Reynolds, Irish Prime Minister

SOCIETY

Our human stock is threatened. These mothers – single parents from classes 4 and 5 – are now producing a third of all births. If we do nothing, the nation moves towards degeneration.

Sir Keith Joseph MP

Citizens make cities, and cities make citizens.

John Prescott MP

The public education system in America is one of the most important foundations of our democracy. After all, it is where children from all over America learn to be responsible citizens, and learn to have the skills necessary to take advantage of our fantastic opportunistic society.

President George W. Bush

Things are more like they are now than they ever were before.

President Dwight D. Eisenhower

Classless society? What is it? Just a ridiculous phrase.

Sir Nicholas Fairbairn MP

I never knew the lower classes had such white skins.

Lord Curzon

SPACE EXPLORATION

Space is almost infinite. As a matter of fact, we think it is infinite.

Vice President Dan Quayle

I am convinced that UFOs exist, because I have seen one.

President Jimmy Carter

There's a lot of uncharted waters in space.

Vice President Dan Quayle

We are leaders of the world of the space programme. We have been the leader of the world of our – of the space programme and we're going to continue with where we're going to go, notwithstanding the Soviet Union's demise and its collapse – the former Soviet Union – we now have independent republics which used to be called the Soviet Union. Space is the new frontier to be explored. And we're going to explore. Think of all the things we rely upon from space today: communications from – Japan, detection of potential ballistic missile attacks. Ballistic missiles are still here. Other nations do have ballistic missiles. How do you think we were able to detect some of the Soviet missiles and things like that? Space, reconnaissance, weather, communications – you name it. We use space a lot today.

Vice President Dan Quayle

A mirror system in space could provide the light equivalent of many full moons so that there would be no need for night-time lighting of the highways. Ambient light covering entire areas could reduce the current danger of criminals lurking in darkness.

Newt Gingrich, Speaker of the House of Representatives

Mars is essentially in the same orbit. Mars is somewhat the same distance from the sun, which is very important. We have seen pictures where there are canals, we believe, and water. If there is water, that means there is oxygen. If oxygen, that means we can breathe.

Vice President Dan Quayle

I've often wondered, what if all of us in the world discovered that we were threatened by an outer – a power from outer space, from another planet?

President Ronald Reagan

For NASA, space is still a high priority.

Vice President Dan Quayle

It's time for the human race to enter the solar system.

Vice President Dan Quayle

Prince Philip: Would you like to travel into space?

Child: Yes.

Prince Philip: Well, you'll have to lose a bit of weight first.

SPIN

David Mellor is in government principally because of his ability to give a good news gloss to any disaster that turns up. He is a man who would have hailed the sinking of the Titanic as a first in underwater exploration. He would have greeted the Black Death as a necessary step towards a leaner and fitter economy. He would have celebrated the Great Fire of London as a vital contribution to urban regeneration.

Bryan Gould MP

SPORT

I love sports. Whenever I can, I always watch the Detroit Tigers on the radio.

President Gerald Ford

So on behalf of a well-oiled unit of people who came together to serve something greater than themselves, congratulations.

President George W. Bush, congratulating the University of Nebraska women's volleyball team

With the retirement of Dickie Bird,
something sad will have gone out of
English cricket.

John Major, Prime Minister

Of course it's great to see Paul Gascoigne
starting at the other team's goal and run the
whole length of the field to score.

Harriet Harman MP

STATESMEN

Mrs Thatcher was a wonderful world
statesman.

Lady Porter

STATISTICS

We said zero, and I think any statistician will
tell you that when you're dealing with very
big numbers, zero must mean plus or minus
a few.

William Waldegrave MP

SUCCESS

If we don't succeed, we run the risk of failure.

Vice President Dan Quayle

It was not a failure. It was an incomplete success.

**President Jimmy Carter, on the failed attempt
to rescue the US embassy hostages in Iran**

I'm hopeful. I know there is a lot of ambition in Washington, obviously. But I hope the ambitious realise that they are more likely to succeed with success as opposed to failure.

President George W. Bush

The road to success is filled with women pushing their husbands along.

Lord Dewar

SUCCESSION

I was my best successor but I decided not to succeed myself.

Pierre Trudeau, Canadian Prime Minister

I think there are many, many people who could replace Margaret Thatcher when she finally hangs up her fighting boots.

Norman Tebbit MP

SUGGESTIONS

While the press is here, was there – did the Democratic governors meet, and is there any feeling that we shouldn't press to try to get something done by March 20th? Do we – is there – can anyone – is there a spokesman on that point? Because what I would like to suggest – not that you'd have to sign every 't' and 'i' but that we urge Congress to move by that date. And if that date isn't good, what date? Is there any feeling on that one?

President George Bush, Sr.

SUPPORT

We experienced a haemorrhoid last year.

Charles Kennedy MP, attempting to say 'haemorrhage'

There was universal support for it, and very little opposition.

Lord Montgomery

If I have any prejudice against the honourable Member, it is in his favour.

Sir Boyle Roche MP

SURPRISE

This is a delightful surprise to the extent that it is a surprise and only a surprise to the extent that we anticipated.

US Secretary of State James Baker

TACTICS

Our intent will not be to create gridlock. Oh, except maybe from time to time.

Senator Bob Dole, on working with the Clinton administration

The door is now open. What we have to do is push it fully ajar.

Elliot Morley MP

TAXATION

Our party has been accused of fooling the public by calling the tax increases 'revenue enhancement'. Not so. No one was fooled.

Vice President Dan Quayle

Far from being a vote loser, with your help it will be a vote winner and launch us on our fourth term.

Michael Portillo MP, on the Poll Tax

I'd like the taxes to go to those parents lucky enough to have children.

Tony Banks MP

The local authorities are caught between the deep blue sea of the rates and the frying pan of the Poll Tax.

Anon. Tory backbencher

A tax cut is really one of the anecdotes to coming out of an economic illness.

President George W. Bush

In all due respect, it is – I'm not sure eighty per cent of the people get death tax. I know this – one hundred per cent will get it if I'm the President.

President George W. Bush

A cow may be drained dry, and if the Chancellors of the Exchequer persist in meeting every deficiency that occurs by taxing the brewing and distilling industries, they will inevitably kill the cow that lays the golden milk.

Sir Frederick Milner MP

TECHNOLOGY

I took the initiative in creating the Internet.

Vice President Al Gore

When will the highways on the Internet become more few?

President George W. Bush

The Internet is a great way to get on the net.

Senator Bob Dole of Kansas, US presidential candidate

Pushed the button down here and one up
here with the green thing on it. And out
came a command to somebody that I had
written.

**President George Bush, Sr., on learning
to use a PC**

TERRORISM

They never stop thinking about new ways to
harm our country and our people, and
neither do we.

President George W Bush on Al Qaeda

The IRA will stick to their guns on
decommissioning.

Gerry Adams MP

We will double our special forces to conduct
terrorist operations.

John Kerry, US presidential candidate

When the IRA plant such bombs, it proves
they can scare people, it proves they can kill
people, it proves nothing.

Peter Bottomley MP

I saw an airplane hit the tower – the TV was obviously on – and I used to fly myself, and I said, 'There's one terrible pilot.'

President George W. Bush

We are not going to stand idly by and be murdered in our beds.

Reverend Ian Paisley MP

September 11 was one of the most brilliantly organised operations in modern history. Anybody who has ever tried to organise a cheese and wine party in a Conservative Association will know how difficult it is.

Sir Peter Tapsell

Thirty injured, nobody dead. At the end of this opera everybody's dead.

Sir Patrick Mayhew MP, responding to journalists' questions about the latest IRA bomb attack, as he was arriving to see Donizetti's Lucia di Lammermoor

The IRA are deadly serious about a cessation of violence.

John Hume MP

If you find a person that you've never seen before getting into a crop duster that doesn't belong to you, report it.

President George W. Bush

It would be the equivalent of having the Prime Minister of England invite the Oklahoma bomber to 10 Downing Street, to congratulate him on a job well done.

Margaret Thatcher, former Prime Minister, on President Clinton's welcome of Sinn Fein leader Gerry Adams to the United States in 1995

That was consciously ambiguous in the sense that any terrorist government or any terrorist movement that is contemplating such actions I think knows clearly what we are speaking of.

Alexander Haig, US Secretary of State

These people doing these murders are masquerading openly in the streets.

Reverend Ian Paisley MP

Friends, fellow Irishmen and Irishwomen, fellow gunmen and gunwomen.

Gerry Adams MP, in 1983

We know of certain knowledge that he is in Afghanistan, or some other county, or dead.

**Donald Rumsfeld on Osama Bin Laden,
in 2002**

The IRA have been isolated in the eyes of the world and many other people.

John Major, Prime Minister

I believe that all illegal organisations should be outlawed.

Reverend Ian Paisley MP

How would I stop the IRA bombing campaign? I'd shoot their planes down!

Ross Perot, US presidential candidate

I have reason to believe that the fowl pest outbreaks are the work of the IRA.

Reverend Ian Paisley MP

The Government will never accept an acceptable level of violence.

Patrick Donegan, Irish politician

It is ludicrous to see Sinn Fein calling for better housing for people of the North while at the same time the IRA are blowing up houses.

Peter Barry, Irish Minister for Foreign Affairs

TEXAS

I was raised in the West – the West of Texas. It's pretty close to California – in more ways than Washington DC is close to California.

President George W. Bush

THREATS

And if he continues that, I'm going to tell the nation what I think of him as a human being and a person.

President George W. Bush

This is John Major's last desperate throw of the dice and we will ensure it scores a double blank.

Jack Straw MP

That low-down scoundrel deserves to be kicked to death by a jackass, and I'm just the one to do it.

Anon. Congressional candidate in Texas

If Lenin's widow does not behave, we shall appoint someone else as Lenin's widow.

Joseph Stalin

TRADE

It's very important for folks to realise that when there's more trade, there's more commerce.

President George W. Bush

It is clear our nation is reliant upon big foreign oil. More and more of our imports come from overseas.

President George W. Bush

Everybody likes to go to Geneva. You'd find these potentates from down in Africa, you know – rather than eating each other, they'd just come up and get a good square meal in Geneva.

Senator Ernest Hollings, on international trade conferences in Geneva

TRADITION

It is better to do something quite absurd for which there is a precedent than to make oneself responsible for an unprecedented act of wisdom.

Arthur Balfour MP

TRANSPORT

Most motorists use roads rather than the Underground or railways.

Stephen Byers MP

You have your own company, your own temperature control, your own music and you don't have to put up with dreadful human beings sitting alongside you.

Steven Norris MP, explaining the benefits of private cars as opposed to public transport

For the first time in fifty years, bus passenger numbers have risen to their highest level ever.

John Prescott MP

The advent of these sleek coaches should provide a tremendous shot in the arm to both legs of Nevada's passenger train system.

Senator Howard Cannon of Nevada

I can't take my chauffeur everywhere.

Derek Laud, Conservative candidate for Tottenham, explaining why he had been caught drink driving

You suddenly realise that you are no longer in government when you get into the back of your car and it doesn't go anywhere.

Sir Malcolm Rifkind MP

Let me make it crystal clear that any privatisation of the railway system which there is on the arrival of a Labour government will be quickly and effectively returned to public ownership.

John Prescott MP, in 1993

TRUST

I never trust a man unless I've got his pecker in my pocket.

President Lyndon B. Johnson

TRUTH

There is not a man, woman or child present through whose mind the truth of what I have just stated has not been ringing for centuries.

Sir Boyle Roche MP

If you won't tell me who told you that, it's not worth the paper it was written on.

Malcolm Rifkind MP

Lloyd George spent his whole life plastering together the true and the false and therefrom manufacturing the plausible.

Stanley Baldwin, Prime Minister

UNEMPLOYMENT

A few years ago everyone was saying we must have more leisure. Now they are complaining they are unemployed. People do not seem to be able to make up their minds, do they?

Prince Philip

Youth unemployment has fell.

Joan Ryan MP

The Alliance will reduce employment by one million in three years.

SDP/Liberal Alliance election leaflet, 1987

Job insecurity is a state of mind.

Ian Lang MP, President of the Board of Trade

I want to thank the dozens of welfare to work stories, the actual examples of people who made the firm and solemn commitment to work hard and embetter themselves.

President George W. Bush

When a great many people are unable to find work, unemployment results.

President Calvin Coolidge

The increase in male unemployment for men between 1966 and 1972 can be fully explained by the almost continuous fall in male employment in this period.

Department of Employment's Employment Gazette, 1976

British unemployment is rising faster here than in any other European country.

Neil Kinnock MP

Dick Cheney and I do not want this nation to be in a recession. We want anybody who can find work to be able to find work.

President George W. Bush

The trend in the rise in unemployment is downward.

Gillian Shepherd MP

We are trying to get unemployment to go up, and I think we're going to succeed.

President Ronald Reagan

I want to make sure that everybody who has a job wants a job.

President George Bush, Sr.

He didn't riot. He got on his bike and looked for work.

Norman Tebbit MP, on his father's experience of unemployment

UNIVERSITIES

The slowing in the universities' rate of expansion experienced in the 1970s was replaced in the early 1980s by an expenditure-led policy of contraction.

Review of the University Grants Commission, a government report on university funding, on spending cuts

We have no business subsidising intellectual curiosity.

President Ronald Reagan

UNITY

Our nation must come together to unite.

President George W. Bush

VICE PRESIDENCY

Interviewer: What will you do if you assume the Vice Presidency?

Dan Quayle: Certainly, I know what to do, and when I am Vice President – and I will be

– there will be contingency plans under different sets of situations, and I tell you what – I'm not going to go out and hold a news conference about it. I'm going to put it in a safe place and keep it there! Does that answer your question?

I am against vice in every form, including the Vice Presidency.

Representative Morris K. Udall of Arizona

VIOLENCE

The US condones violence in El Salvador.

Vice President Dan Quayle

VOTES

Votes are like trees, if you're trying to build a forest. If you have more trees than you have forests, then at that point the pollsters will probably say you will win.

Vice President Dan Quayle

If my own mother had been alive, even she would not have voted for me.

Representative Mickey Edwards of Oklahoma

Even a right-wing moron in a hurry would feel completely unembarrassed to vote for us.

Tony Banks MP

This ain't the easiest job in the world. Listen, here's the final word. Vote for me. Don't vote for them. Vote for me, okay?

President George Bush, Sr.

The voters have spoken – the bastards.

President Richard Nixon

Interviewer: Why did you fail to hold on to your seat?

Sean Doherty: Not enough people voted for me.

If you vote for Kinnock, you are voting against Christ.

Dame Barbara Cartland, 1992

I can tell you exactly how many trade union members voted for the SDP – about twenty per cent.

Shirley Williams MP

It's no exaggeration to say that the undecideds could go one way or another.

President George Bush, Sr.

I always vote for the Tories. They are my best clients.

Norma Levy, prostitute involved in the Lord Lambton scandal in 1973

A low voter turnout is an indication of fewer people going to the polls.

Vice President Dan Quayle

VOTING SYSTEMS

The United States, which has a similar type of voting system as ourselves, but very different ...

David Owen MP

Americans have the best system in the world. They've just got to find a way to make it work.

Vice President Nelson Rockefeller

WALES

They're all the same. They're short, they're fat and they are fundamentally corrupt.

Rod Richards MP, junior Welsh Office minister, on Welsh Labour councillors

WARFARE

They are retreating on all fronts. Their military effort is a subject of laughter throughout the world.

Mohammed Saeed al-Sahaf, Iraqi Minister of Information, on the American military action

The United States has so much to offer the Third World War.

President Ronald Reagan

We are not at war with Egypt. We are in an armed conflict.

Sir Anthony Eden, Prime Minister

I triple guarantee you, there are no American soldiers in Baghdad.

Mohammed Saeed al-Sahaf, Iraqi Minister of Information

No matter what happens, the US Navy is not going to be caught napping.

Frank Knox, Secretary of the Navy, three days before the Japanese attack on Pearl Harbour

The war situation has developed, not necessarily to Japan's advantage.

Japanese Emperor Hirohito, announcing Japanese surrender in 1945

We are going to have peace even if we have to fight for it.

President Dwight D. Eisenhower

To be a great President, you have to have a war. All the great Presidents have had their wars.

William J. Crowe, US Admiral

It became necessary to destroy the village in order to save it.

US Army report on the destruction of Ben Tre, South Vietnam, in 1968

We should declare war on North Vietnam. We could pave the whole country and put parking stripes on it, and still be home by Christmas.

Governor Ronald Reagan of California, 1966

Let's try to settle this problem like good Christians.

Warren Austin, US delegate to the United Nation, on the Arab-Israeli war

An alarm was given that a gang of rebels in full retreat were advancing under the French standard. They had no colours nor any drums except bagpipes.

Sir Boyle Roche MP

A dispute over the sovereignty of that little ice-cold bunch of land down there.

President Ronald Reagan, on the Falklands War

They would never agree to peace so long as Prussian militarism held its head above water to trample underfoot our liberties.

Sir Edward Carson

It was part of the fortunes of war. We didn't have counsellors rushing around every time somebody let off a gun, asking, 'Are you all right? Are you sure you don't have a ghastly problem?' You just got on with it.

Prince Philip, commenting on the Second World War

Nuclear war is something that may not be desirable.

Ed Messe, counsellor in Reagan's administration

WARNINGS

This is a man who will stoop at nothing.

Sir Ivan Lawrence MP

If this thing starts to snowball, it will catch fire right across the country.

**Robert Thompson, former Social Credit
leader in Canada**

If you let that sort of thing go on, your bread and butter will be cut out right from under your feet.

Ernest Bevin MP

This could well be the goose that killed the golden egg.

Anon. Chester city councillor

It would be like sticking my head in a moose.

Mayor Allan Lamport of Toronto

We don't want to see these coal fields trampled into the ground.

**Rodney Bickerstaff, General Secretary of the
National Union of Public Employees**

Be assured. Baghdad is safe, protected.

**Mohammed Saeed al-Sahaf, Iraqi
Minister of Information**

WEAPONS

I do not like this word 'bomb'. It is not a bomb. It is a device that is exploding.

Jacques le Blanc, French ambassador to New Zealand, commenting on France's nuclear tests in the Pacific

Atomic energy might be as good as our present-day explosives, but it's unlikely to produce anything much more dangerous.

Winston Churchill in 1939

You always write it's bombing, bombing, bombing. It is not bombing. It's air support.

Colonel David Opfer, US Air Force attaché at the American embassy in Cambodia, to journalists in 1974

We are getting cruise missiles more accurate so that we can have precise precision.

Vice President Dan Quayle

I want to lob one into the men's room of the Kremlin and make sure I hit it.

Barry Goldwater, Republican presidential candidate, on nuclear weapons, 1964

I don't want nations feeling like that they can bully ourselves and our allies. I want to have a ballistic defence system so that we can make the world more peaceful, and at the same time I want to reduce our own nuclear capabilities to the level commiserate with keeping the peace.

President George W. Bush

We will create new Hiroshimas and Nagasakis. I will not hesitate to deploy nuclear weapons. You know what Chernobyl meant for our country. You will get your own Chernobyl in Germany.

Vladimir Zhirinovsky, Russian nationalist

We are conducting limited duration protective reaction air strikes.

Anon. US Army spokesman, describing a bombing campaign in Vietnam

If we're going to maintain America's status as the number one maritime power, it means having modern musicians and well-trained sailors.

Governor Michael Dukakis of Massachusetts, attempting to say 'modern munitions'

If we have to start over again with another Adam and Eve, I want them to be Americans and not Russians.

Senator Richard Russell of Georgia, on nuclear holocaust

I wanted to educate the American people to lose some of their fear of the word 'nuclear'. When you say 'nuclear', all the American people see is a mushroom cloud. But for military purposes, it's just enough firepower to get the job done.

Barry Goldwater, Republican presidential candidate, 1964

My fellow Americans, I've signed legislation that will outlaw Russia forever. We begin bombing in five minutes.

President Ronald Reagan, about to go on the air for a radio broadcast, unaware that the microphone was already on

Wait a minute! I'm not interested in agriculture. I want the military stuff.

Senator William Scott, during a briefing in which officials began telling him about missile silos

You might be interested to know that the scriptures are on our side in relation to the arms build-up.

President Ronald Reagan

WELFARE STATE

The welfare state kills more poor people in a year than private business.

Newt Gingrich, Speaker of the House of Representatives

WISDOM

What a waste it is to lose one's mind. Or not to have a mind is being very wasteful. How true that is.

Vice President Dan Quayle

Let us hope and trust that there are sufficient proud and ignorant people left in this country to stand up to the intellectuals who are out to destroy faith and fatherland.

Oliver J. Flanagan, Irish politician

I'm not what you call your basic intellectual.

President George Bush, Sr.

WIVES

Things have come to a pretty pass when an Englishman may not have his wife backwards and forwards.

Sir Robert Inglis MP, commenting on prisoners' visiting rights in 1851

WOMEN

Women don't vote for women. Most of them vote for me.

Bertie Ahern, Irish Prime Minister

At least fifty per cent of the population are women, and the rest men.

Harriet Harman MP

Sensible and responsible women do not want to vote.

President Grover Cleveland

Of course we are not patronising women. We are just going to explain to them in words of one syllable what it is all about.

Lady Olga Maitland MP

If a competent and suitable woman was appointed to the British Railways Board, more attention would be paid to cleaning up the stations.

Lady Ward

Mothers should encourage their daughters as much as their sons to take up physics and maths. And if they find them difficult, she should say, 'Well, daddy will help you.'

Lady Platt

You drag $100 bills through trailer parks, there's no telling what you'll find. I know these people. I went to school with them. I necked with them in back seats, spent nights with them.

James Carville, campaign adviser to Bill Clinton, on women who claimed they had sex with Bill Clinton

The greatest thing for any woman is to be a wife and mother.

Theodore Roosevelt

They seem to be saying, 'Here, I've got breasts. Vote for me.'

Larry Yatch, former Pennsylvanian Democratic Party chairman, on female candidates

Women MPs don't give me feelings of femininity. They lack fragrance. They're definitely not desert island material. They all look as though they're from the Fifth Kiev Stalinist machine gun parade. As for Edwina Currie, well, the only person who smells her fragrance is herself. I can't stand the hag.

Sir Nicholas Fairbairn MP

I think it's about time we voted for senators with breasts. After all, we've been voting for boobs long enough.

Claire Sargent, a senatorial candidate in Arizona

What is a skirt but an open gateway?

Sir Nicholas Fairbairn MP

WORK

There remain only twenty-five hours in the day, and Neil Kinnock is already working for twenty-three of them.

Robin Cook MP

I personally favour mandatory requirement of work for everybody, including women with young children.

Newt Gingrich, Speaker of the House of Representatives

WORLD

The world has gone through a tremendous change recently, both nationally and internationally.

John Major, Prime Minister

We're part of a global world these days.

Brian Chamberlain, New Zealand agricultural trade special representative

YOUTH

Young people by definition have their future before them.

Neil Kinnock MP

John Redwood is a young man but, let's face it, so was Margaret Thatcher in 1975.

Edward Leigh MP

INDEX